CHRISTIAN DE

# THE
# POWER
# OF
# GOD'S WORD

## FOR
## RECEIVING HEALING

### VOLUME 2

VITAL KEYS
TO VICTORY OVER SICKNESS

BY ANNE B. BUCHANAN

The Power of God's Word for Receiving Healing: Vital Keys to Victory Over Sickness (Christian Devotional Healing Series, Volume 2)
Copyright © 2011, 2012 by Anne B. Buchanan

## Disclaimer / Limitations of Liability

All material in this book is for information and educational purposes only. No information concerning matters of health is intended as a means to diagnose or treat diseases. No information is intended to be a substitute for medical advice by a licensed health care provider. All readers should consult a licensed health care provider and The Great Physician in all matters relating to medical problems, especially in matters of diagnosing or treating diseases or other physical and mental conditions. The Author and Publisher do not directly or indirectly give medical advice, nor do they prescribe any supplements or assume any responsibility or liability for those who treat themselves. No statements in this publication have been analyzed or approved by the FDA.

Dedicated

To The Glory of God
Who Loves Us
And Who Heals Us




In Memory of
My mother, Elizabeth

# Table of Contents

## Great Resources

# ✝

# PREFACE

This is Volume 2 of *The Power of God's Word* Series. We continue to explore the vital keys to manifesting victory in defeating sickness and disease. The Word of God is exciting, and few topics are more life-changing than revelations on healing and being made whole through the precious blood of Jesus. We will press in deeper to learn what Jesus really did for us on the Cross and how to exercise the authority He won for us.

Remember that the foundations for many of the Biblical principles that we discuss in these devotions were laid in Volume 1, *The Power of God's Word for Healing*. Therefore, you will get the most out of this book if you have read Volume 1 first.

A major turning point in my learning journey came when I discovered the meaning of the Greek word "*sozo,*" which is translated "save" in English. Because I did not know the Greek language, I always missed the full impact of what the Holy Spirit was saying in numerous scriptures. Once I was introduced to the *Strong's Concordance* and I could examine any word in the Bible, an entirely new level of revelation opened up to me.

The Greek word "*sozo*" means "to save, heal, deliver, and make whole." Therefore, it expresses far more than the English translation, "save," conveys. I went through the New Testament and searched for every place where I saw the word "save." I looked in my concordance to see if the Greek word was "*sozo*," and, if so, I wrote the full meaning of the word in the margin of my Bible. When I re-read the passage of scripture using the full meaning, I was astonished at the message that God was telling me.

I am sharing that revelation with you in this book and hope that it will be as uplifting and illuminating for you as it has been for me. In this book you will learn about God's healing power and how to be made whole through the precious blood of Jesus. It is all about learning what Jesus *really* did for us on the Cross and how to exercise the authority He won for us.

In my own personal life, I find that God's Word and God's remedies make a powerful combination for healing. The God who created me also created the plants, herbs, and essential oils, and I believe He did so with full *intention* – knowing exactly how my body works and how these natural substances meet my bodily needs. However, I want to emphasize that I never forget that it is the Creator who is to be exalted, not the creation. It is the Lord God Almighty who is my Healer, rather than any substance which I may use temporarily to assist my bodily functions to return to a proper balance.

Each person has to take full responsibility for his own health and make his own personal decision about medical care. Those who are on medications need to be particularly cautious. Some medications create a serious physical dependency in the natural world and to discontinue them suddenly can lead to rapid death unless God intervenes supernaturally. God's Word tells us we are not to tempt Him.

Therefore, to discontinue any medication in a rush of "instant faith" would most likely be a fatal decision that would delight the evil one. Don't do it. Instead, strengthen your faith, pray with your medical counselors, and seek God's instruction and your doctor's instructions about what changes to make and when to make them. I am not a medical doctor and do not prescribe or suggest any medical treatments. Please heed the disclaimer at the beginning of this book and seek appropriate health care professionals in matters concerning your health.

Please note that I have occasionally taken a few liberties with the English language in this book. I have bent a few rules of grammar so that what you read matches the way that people speak. I have also intentionally spelled satan's name with a small "s" except at the beginning of a sentence. Writing his name in lower case provides a visual reminder that he has been totally defeated by our Risen Savior and has only the power we choose to give him.

This book proclaims God's healing power in small daily doses, boosting our faith step by step and reminding us of God's Holy Word and His covenant with us. It is easy to talk about faith and quite another to navigate the path of healing with focus and purpose. I hope that all who read these messages will be blessed by them.

At the end of the book are a few selected references to materials which you may find useful if you wish to explore further. I am very grateful for those who have long proclaimed God's healing message and who have been instrumental in helping me along the way.

If you like this volume of *The Power of God's Word*, please check out the other volumes in the series, which are available in paperback, on Kindle, on Nook, and as PDF downloadable files. In addition, there are full sets of scripture cards available. Complete ordering information is on my website: http://www.PowerofGodsWord.com.

If you need personal prayer and support, please join our community of believers at our blog website which has many resources available. You will find great articles on numerous topics related to healing, tutorials on free online Bible search websites, video of healing testimonies, and links to a free online downloads of some of these devotions as audio files.

Share your questions, thoughts, and victories with us and get support for your own journey in healing in a safe environment of like-minded believers. You will find us at: http://www.Godwantsyoutobewell.com

Many blessings to each one of you,

Anne Buchanan

✝

# Day 1
# Jehovah Is the God Who Heals You

*... I am the Lord Who heals you.* (Exodus 15:26 *Amplified Bible*)

When Moses asked God who He was, God replied, "I AM who I AM" which is translated Yahweh or Jehovah. Later in Holy Scripture, God reveals Himself and His divine essence by using seven more detailed additions to His name.

One of them is Jehovah-Rapha (the Lord who heals us) which is given in Exodus 15. The Hebrew word *"rapha"* means to mend, cure, heal, repair, and make whole. It also can be translated as "physician." Thus, Father God declares Himself to be our Great Physician. He mends us, cures us, repairs us, and makes us whole. He is the one who created us and He desires for us to walk in His divine health.

How wonderful it is that one of the most important things that God wanted us to know about Him was that He is a healer. He created Adam and Eve without sickness, and it was only after they came to know evil through their choice of disobedience that they were subject to illness and disease.

Since God's plan was revealed in the Garden of Eden, we know that sickness was not part of God's plan for man. It was part of satan's plan to separate man from God. But God is infinitely more powerful than satan. Hallelujah!

God knows how devastating illness can be. So He covenants with us that He has the power to make His plan prevail. He is always perfectly faithful to us. Psalm 107:20 says, "He sent His Word and healed them." God did indeed send His Son so that we could be fully redeemed, saved, delivered, and healed in our spirit, our soul, and our body. Jesus carried not only our sins to Calvary's Cross but also our illnesses.

No matter what sickness or infirmity may befall us, we are healed by the stripes and blood of Jesus. Receive your healing now.

*Almighty God, I give you grateful thanks for revealing Yourself as Jehovah-Rapha, my Great Physician and the mighty God who heals me. I am so thankful that You are above all sickness and disease. In the name of Jesus, I command every malfunctioning cell, tissue, gland, and organ to perform perfectly. You are the God who calls what is not as though it were, so I proclaim with confidence that every cell in my body is healthy and whole according to Your holy Word. I apply the blood of Jesus to every organ and speak life and vitality to each one. I receive my healing now in the mighty name of Jesus Christ, my Savior and my Redeemer, Amen.*

†

# DAY 2
# THE IMPORTANCE OF THE GREEK WORD "SOZO"

*If we this day be examined of the good deed done to the impotent man, by what means he is made whole [sozo]; Be it known unto you all ... that by the name of Jesus Christ of Nazareth, whom ye crucified, whom God raised from the dead, even by him doth this man stand here before you whole. This is the stone which was set at nought of you builders, which is become the head of the corner. Neither is there salvation in any other: for there is none other name under heaven given among men, whereby we must be saved [sozo]. (Acts 4:9-12)*

Peter healed a crippled man and he got into trouble for it. The rulers, elders, and teachers of the law called Peter before them for questioning in order to stop the healings from happening again and to find out the source of his power. Peter told them plainly that his power came from Jesus, who God had raised from the dead.

Verse 12 is an important one. "Neither is there salvation in any other: for there is none other name under heaven given among men, whereby we must be saved." The Greek word translated as "salvation" is "*soteria*," which means rescue, safety, deliverance, salvation, and health. The last word in the sentence is the Greek word "*sozo*", which means to save, deliver, protect, heal, and be made whole.

Notice that being saved and being healed are bound together in the meaning of the Greek word *"sozo"* just as Jesus repeatedly bound them together in his description of His mission and purpose and in His instructions to all His followers for *their* mission and *their* purpose.

Accept the salvation that God has offered to you. Praise God that you have been given salvation for your spirit, your precious eternal self. But recognize, accept, and believe that the other benefits included in the Greek word *"sozo"* (healing, deliverance, and being made whole) have been provided for your *entire* being, which includes your mind and your body as well. Jesus paid an awesome price for you, so receive with gratitude and thanksgiving all His gifts of salvation, deliverance, and healing.

*Dear Father, thank You for revealing to me what "sozo" means. I thank You that I am saved and healed and delivered and made whole. My wholeness of spirit, soul, and body is Your divine will, and I rejoice in Your abundant provision for me. Thank You for sending Your Son to redeem me. I accept all these blessings, Father. I accept Your salvation, Your rescue, Your deliverance, and Your healing. Thank You, Father, for Your mercy and Your blessings. In the name of Jesus Christ, my Savior and my Redeemer, I pray, Amen.*

†

# Day 3
# The Truth Makes You Free

*And ye shall know the truth, and the truth shall make you free.*
*(John 8:32)*

God has always wanted us to be free. From the very beginning He gave us free will so that we would enter into relationship with Him voluntarily out of our desire to do so and for no other reason.

When we disobeyed Him and ruined the plan, our Heavenly Father sent Jesus to reclaim us and to remove the bonds of the evil one. Jesus set us free, and He told us how to remain free by living in the truth. Satan can't tolerate the truth because the truth is God manifested.

The truth is especially crucial to our healing. Since sickness itself is a tool of the father of lies, we are especially vulnerable to deceptive appearances when we feel ill. The truth is often difficult to accept, and sometimes it is impossible to "prove." Even though "facts" are real, they often do not reflect God's truth.

In court, we are asked to tell "the truth, the whole truth, and nothing but the truth." Yet with illness we are deceived into looking at the physical level only, even though that is not the *whole* truth. To see the *whole* truth we must look to things unseen, and we are called to depend on God's faith rather than man's scientific "facts."

19

To be free from sickness we must know the truth about it. And what is that truth? That its source is the evil one. That it is not part of God's will for us. That it has been borne on the Cross by Jesus Christ. That the stripes of Jesus have paid the full price for every illness. That God wants us to be free from the bondage of disease.

Immerse yourself in the living Word of the Holy Scriptures. Since the Holy Spirit was sent to us as a beacon of truth, He has a vital role to play in the choices that we make. Take your health questions to God. One by one place your questions at the feet of Jesus, and then ask the Holy Spirit to reveal God's answers to you. Be very specific in your questions and after asking each question be quiet and listen.

You will know the truth, and the truth shall make you free.

*Gracious God, I walk gladly into the sunshine of Your truth, goodness, and mercy. It is through Your love and Your compassion that I am healed by the stripes of Jesus. Keep me always centered in Your perfect truth, which lights my way, makes me free from the bondage of the father of lies, and keeps me grounded in Your healing love. I give You grateful thanks for the blessings of life, joy, and abundant health. In the name of the Father, the Son, and the Holy Spirit, I pray, Amen.*

✝

# DAY 4
# IT IS GOD'S WILL FOR YOU TO BE WELL

*And there came a leper to him , beseeching him, and kneeling down to him, and saying unto him, If thou wilt, thou canst make me clean.*

*And Jesus, moved with compassion, put forth his hand, and touched him, and saith unto him, I will: be thou clean. And as soon as he had spoken, immediately the leprosy departed from him, and he was cleansed. (Mark 1:40-42)*

It is interesting to note that there are only a couple of places recorded in Holy Scripture where someone comes to Jesus for healing and does not assume that Jesus will heal him. Here we see the man with leprosy saying, "if you will, you can make me clean."

Notice the response of Jesus. He was filled with compassion for the man, and immediately reached out to touch him, saying, "I will. I am willing."

Since Jesus was the perfect expression of God's will, every one of His acts and statements reflected the will of Jehovah. With regard to healing, Jesus left no one sick for any reason. Therefore, when the leper came questioning Jesus' will to heal him, Jesus wanted to make sure that that issue was settled immediately. "I am willing. Be clean."

21

"If it be thy will" is a completely appropriate prayer when you are trying to determine if you should move to a certain city, marry a certain person, or choose a certain career. These answers depend on your listening for God's guidance and are not found in the Holy Scripture.

But God's healing will *is* declared in Holy Scripture, and the actions of Christ Jesus fulfilled God's Word perfectly by healing *everyone* who came to be made well. "And great multitudes followed him, and he healed them *all*" (Matthew 12:15). "And Jesus went about all Galilee, teaching in their synagogues, and preaching the gospel of the kingdom, and healing *all* manner of sickness and *all* manner of disease among the people" (Matthew 4:23).

We can rejoice with an exuberant heart knowing that our God not only says "I will" but also says "I already have." We know that by the stripes of Jesus we were healed and so we are!

*Loving Father God, I come with joy in my heart and praise on my lips. I don't have to come to You wondering if You will heal me. I proclaim the glory of the life, death, and resurrection of Jesus, my Savior, who took the stripes on His back and from the Cross said, "It is finished." From the moment that Jesus bore every sickness and ailment, Your healing power has been flowing to every believer. I am a believer, Father, and I receive my healing now. In Jesus' name, I pray, Amen.*

✝

# DAY 5
## JESUS BORE YOUR SINS AND YOUR SICKNESSES

*Who his own self bare our sins in his own body on the tree, that we, being dead to sins, should live unto righteousness: by whose stripes ye were healed.*

*For ye were as sheep going astray; but are now returned unto the Shepherd and Bishop of your souls.   (1 Peter 2:24-25)*

"By His stripes you have been healed."   Hallelujah! Repeat out loud three times, "By His stripes I was healed." "By His stripes I was healed." "By His stripes I was healed." It has already been done.  Receive it, because it has already been done.  What you are seeking now is to line up with God so that you can experience the fulfillment of His Word and see the manifestation of your healing.

Healing of the body alone means nothing if your spirit is in jeopardy because you aren't saved.  That's the reason that Jesus came to bear both our sins and our infirmities.  The healing of body and spirit was part of Jesus' mission.  He said to the teachers of the law who opposed Him, "Whether is easier, to say, Thy sins be forgiven thee; or to say, Rise up and walk?" (Luke 5:23).  When He spoke both the words of forgiveness *and* the words of healing to a paralytic, the paralytic was healed.

Jesus bore our sins in His body on the tree. That happened two thousand years ago, before you were even born. Jesus said it was finished then. Therefore, when you were born again, you received forgiveness for your sins.

What about the sins you commit now, after your salvation? Contrary to what most Christians believe, there isn't a separate category of sins before salvation and after salvation. Jesus' atonement covered all sins. All of the them.

That is the reason that Peter says we are "dead to sins." Does that mean that it doesn't matter if you do things that are wrong? No. Any sin becomes a door for the enemy to take advantage of you. So repent of it, make a decision not to repeat it, thank the Lord for His forgiveness, and renew your will to live in closer relationship to the Lord.

We have been claimed by our Shepherd. We were as sheep going astray, but we have been found, saved, and healed through His immense, loving sacrifice.

*Lord God Almighty, thank You for sending Your Son, Jesus Christ, to bear my sins in His body on the tree, so that I might die to my sins and live for righteousness. By His stripes I was healed! I was like a sheep going astray, but now I have been returned to You, my shepherd and overseer of my soul. I rejoice in Your great love and the redeeming power of the blood of Jesus. In Jesus' name, I pray, Amen.*

† 

# DAY 6
## BEWARE THE TRADITIONS OF MEN

*Beware lest any man spoil you [take you captive] through philosophy and vain deceit, after the tradition of men, after the rudiments of the world, and not after Christ.* (Colossians 2:8)

Do not be taken captive by beliefs that you accept as God's truth only because you have heard people repeat them so much. One of the most prevalent and devastating ideas is that God causes us to be sick. Satan rejoices in the tradition of men that proclaims that it is not God's will to heal everyone. This is "a philosophy and empty deceit" and depends on the basic principles of this world rather than on Christ.

When you feel tempted to believe this tradition (this "empty deceit"), remember that Jesus brought a new and better covenant to us. Focus on Him. Look at His life. When did He ever see someone who was hurting and refuse to touch him with His healing hand? When did He ever see someone who was blind and refuse to bring him sight? When did He ever pass a cripple and refuse to extend His hand and raise him to his feet?

Never once did Jesus leave people sick because it was God's will that they be ill. Not one single time. The only times it is recorded that Jesus did not heal sick people were

THE POWER OF GOD'S WORD FOR RECEIVING HEALING

times when it was clearly stated that the problem was the people's own disbelief and failure to accept Him.

Not one single time do we ever see Jesus making someone sick because it was God's will that the person suffer and learn a lesson. Not one single time did Jesus cause illness and disease. Not once. Jesus said, "The Son can do nothing of himself, but what he seeth the Father do: for what things soever he doeth, these also doeth the Son likewise" (John 5:19). If it is true that the Father makes people sick, wouldn't Jesus have "done likewise" at least some of the time?

Do not let satan deceive you. Follow the traditions of Jesus and not the traditions of men. "Beware lest any man take you captive through philosophy and empty deceit, according to the tradition of men, according to the basic principles of the world, and not according to Christ."

*Almighty God, in the past I have gotten caught up in philosophies and empty deceits that depend on human tradition and the basic principles of this world. I now focus only on Your Word and Your truth. I affirm that You have made it clear that it is Your will that I be well. So, Father, let Your will be done on earth in my body and in my life as it is in heaven. I refuse to look at my infirmities, to let fear take hold, or to become the captive of the evil one. Thank You, Father, for healing me. In the name of Your Son, Jesus Christ, my Savior and my Redeemer, I pray, Amen.*

† 

# Day 7
## Focus On God's Word

*My son, attend to my words; incline thine ear unto my sayings. Let them not depart from thine eyes; keep them in the midst of thine heart. For they are life unto those that find them, and health to all their flesh.* (Proverbs 4:20-22)

God's prescription for healing is this: if you want your healing to be manifested and if you want to stay healed, listen to His Words and integrate them in the deepest part of your heart and soul. Then you will have health to all your flesh.

James warns us not to be "double-minded" by believing a little and doubting a lot. Here in Proverbs we are told essentially the same thing. God wants one hundred percent focus on Him. If we have our eyes on our symptoms most of the time, we are not looking at the Almighty.

God's Word consistently guides us to life. Our symptoms (which are manifestations of the handiwork of the evil one) lead us to death. We cannot look at these two destinations at the same time.

In this Scripture in Proverbs are there any exceptions listed for healing? Are there any qualifications given? Does it say health to all their flesh except, of course, for incurable diseases? Maybe not for brain cancer. Or multiple sclerosis. Or Alzheimer's disease. There are no exceptions listed or even suggested. God's Word plainly says, "health to *all* their flesh."

And look at the interesting choice of words about the connection between God's Word and life. *To those who find them,* God's Words are life. To those who *find* them. God always requires that we look for Him, that we choose Him. The good news is that He is always available, never hiding.

God never forces us to believe in Him or to follow Him or to be obedient to Him. He simply says, "Here I am. I am the beginning and the end. All power is mine. With Me nothing is impossible."

So we must seek after God. We are told to look for Him in Holy Scripture and to integrate His Word into our hearts and our total being so that we are filled with faith in Him. When that happens, there is no room for the seeds of the evil one to grow, there is no room for doubt, and there is no room for illness. Look to your Heavenly Father and you shall live.

*Almighty God, I love my Bible and I choose to attend to Your words. I incline my ears, my heart, and my soul to Your sayings, and I memorize them and plant them deep within my heart. I know that Your Holy Word is life to me and health to all my flesh. Thank You, Father God, for the gift of Your Word and for the gift of Your Son, who is the Word and who took the stripes on His back for my healing. In Jesus' name, I pray, Amen.*

† 

# DAY 8
## SAY WHAT YOU WANT

*... God, who quickeneth the dead, and calleth those things which be not as though they were.*   (Romans 4:17)

What does it mean to call things that are not as though they were?  You start with the absence of something, and you speak that "missing something" until it is manifested. When you feel sick, it means that you have illness and disease in your body.  What you are missing is health.  So use the principle Jesus taught of having the focused, concentrated faith of a mustard seed and speak health and wellness as though they are present in your body.

Are you one of those people who says, "I call it like I see it?"  If you do that with your health, then your health will always be just exactly the way you keep seeing it.  If you declare yourself to be a cancer victim, then so it is and so it will be.  If you declare yourself to be a diabetic, then so it is and so it will be.  If you declare yourself to be disabled by a stroke, then so it is and so it will be.

As long as you are focused on the way "things are" and the way they appear to be, you are being deceived by satan that God's truth does not exist.  God is the essence of "things unseen" rather than things seen.

Isn't speaking "what is not" just playing pretend and being foolish?  Absolutely not.  This is applying a fundamental principle of faith that is critical for your recovery. It requires you to become part of God's creative process, and it makes you a partner with God for your healing. You do not say, "I have not been diagnosed with diabetes," but you do say, "I call my pancreas functioning normally and my blood sugar levels normal, in Jesus' name." Do you see the difference?

Along with speaking your health, ask God for His guidance. Is there something at the physical level that He wants you to do to participate in the healing process with Him? Pray and then be quiet so that you can hear God's voice clearly. You may be told to use herbs or you may be told to seek certain medical treatment or you may be told to release bitterness and resentments or you may be told simply to receive your healing.

There are multitudes of options available, and God knows what you need so that your healing can be manifested. Go to your Heavenly Father. Ask believing that you have already received your healing. Let Him speak to you through the Holy Spirit and reveal your path to you.

*Loving Father, I stand on Your Holy Word and see myself as You see me, whole and complete. I declare that by the stripes of Jesus I am healed. I proclaim the victory of the Cross and the finished work of salvation, healing, deliverance, and being made whole. I call myself healed because the Word says I am healed. I call every organ in my body whole and well because the Word says that Jesus took my illnesses and sicknesses on Himself. I rejoice in the victory that You purchased for me. In Jesus' name, I pray, Amen.*

†

# DAY 9
## JESUS IS YOUR HEALER

*And Jesus departed from thence, and came nigh unto the sea of Galilee; and went up into a mountain, and sat down there. And great multitudes came unto him, having with them those that were lame, blind, dumb, maimed, and many others, and cast them down at Jesus' feet; and he healed them: Insomuch that the multitude wondered, when they saw the dumb to speak, the maimed to be whole, the lame to walk, and the blind to see: and they glorified the God of Israel.  (Matthew 15:29-31)*

Have you ever thought it would have been wonderful to have lived in Galilee two thousand years ago so that you could have been alive when Jesus was on earth?  Let's create a little movie, going back in time for a moment.

You are sitting on your front step, feeling sick and hopeless.  You hear a lot of noise and see a man going up into the mountains with a great crowd of people following Him.  "Is it the man from Nazareth?" you wonder.  "Is it the man they call Jesus?"

Someone runs by, and you call out to him, asking him your question.  He turns briefly and with a great smile, says, "Yes, it's Jesus.  Come on. Hurry!  Jesus works miracles.  Hurry!"

You get up and join the crowd going to the mountainside.  "I'm just one person in a great crowd," you

31

think as you find a place to sit down. "There's no way I can get close to Him. There are so many people here, He will never even see me, much less heal me." Suddenly there He is, coming right toward you. He squats down and gazes into your eyes with the most compassionate and loving look you have ever seen. He reaches out and takes your hand in His. And you are healed. Sounds good, doesn't it?

But do you realize that it is better for you living now in the twenty-first century? Unlike the people in Galilee, we know Jesus as our victorious Risen Lord. As born-again believers, we have the benefits of His power and love without any limitations whatsoever. We don't have to wait until He comes to our town, and we don't have to push through crowds to get to Him.

Oh, yes, we have it so much better than the people in Galilee. Every moment of every day in every place where we are, we have the shed blood of the Cross as our new covenant. By His stripes we *were* healed. We have the absolute certainty and confidence that Jesus paid every price for us and purchased for us the total package of what the Greek word "*sozo*" means for us – salvation, healing, deliverance, and being made whole. But like the people in Galilee we receive our healing and glorify God.

*Heavenly Father, Your Son is the risen Christ, who died for my sins and my infirmities. Your Holy Scripture says that many crowds came to Him, bringing their sick, and that He healed them all. I have the finished work of the Cross and I rejoice because I was healed by Jesus' stripes. In Jesus' name, I pray, Amen.*

†

# DAY 10
# KEYS TO YOUR HEALING

*That word, I say, ye know, which was published throughout all Judaea, and began from Galilee, after the baptism which John preached; How God anointed Jesus of Nazareth with the Holy Ghost and with power: who went about doing good, and healing all that were oppressed of the devil; for God was with him. (Acts 10:37-38)*

In just one sentence Luke makes an astonishing number of important points that are keys to your healing. He begins by saying that God anointed Jesus. With what? The Holy Spirit and power.

Here is the Greek word *"dunamis"* meaning power, ability, mighty work, strength, and miracle. Because of Jesus' sacrifice for you, that anointing is available to every born-again believer. This anointing wasn't just for Jesus. It wasn't just for the early Christians. It was for all those who take up the Cross and follow Him.

Jesus went around among the people. Doing what? Doing good and healing. Here we see His mission described as being made up of two things – doing good and healing. Healing whom? Healing *all*. Notice that little word "all." Over and over and over again you will see this word used in scripture with regard to healing. Jesus healed them all.

And what conditions was Jesus healing? He was healing problems resulting from people being "oppressed of the devil." Who is the father of disease? Luke makes it very clear that the source of illness is the evil one and that Jesus removed the devil's power.

Jesus overcame all sickness, and, when He took your illnesses to the Cross, He conquered the devil's power and then gave you the responsibility to take authority over the enemy until the day comes when Father God sends the devil into the fire forever. So resist the devil and make him flee.

Jesus accomplished everything He did because He was anointed with power by the Holy Spirit. As a born-again believer, you are anointed with that same power. Use that power for God's glory just as Jesus did. Allow that anointing to work *in* you for your own healing – and also *through* you as you become an instrument for healing and deliverance for others.

*Heavenly Father, I want to be all that You want me to be. I have said yes to the call of Your Son, Jesus Christ and have also received the baptism of the Holy Spirit. I desire to walk in the fullness of all the gifts that You have prepared for me. I want to follow the example of Your Son and be an instrument for the healing of others. I resist satan always and, as a faithful disciple, bring deliverance in the name of Jesus to those oppressed by the devil. Thank You for Your many mercies and Your healing grace that is made manifest in my body. In Jesus' name, I pray, Amen.*

†

# DAY 11
## CAST YOUR CARES ON THE LORD

*Cast thy burden upon the Lord, and he shall sustain thee: he shall never suffer the righteous to be moved.   (Psalm 55:22)*

The Lord will take your burdens (if you give them to Him), hold you up, and never let you down.  Most people say they believe this is true, yet they never actually release their burdens to the Lord.  How can you tell if you have given your cares to the Lord?  By the amount of peace in your soul.

Experiencing illness is different from other problems of life because a wrong decision (or series of decisions) can cost us our lives, and, if that happens, all the other issues which we thought were so important simply end.  Too often we permit all decisions about our treatment and recovery to be made solely by humans, either ourselves or others.  Then when we get deep into a treatment process and it isn't going well, we ask for God's help and prayers from others.

Psalm 55 exhorts us to get our priorities straight.  Cast your cares on the Lord.  Turn to God *first*.  Ask at each step along the way what you should do.  At the first symptom or at the first sign that something is different in your body, turn to God and His Word.  Do what He has commanded you and take authority over the attack of the enemy right then.  If we would do that, illnesses would not progress to a life-threatening stage.

God wants us to be well and He sustains us. He sent His Son to die on the Cross to save us not only by providing eternal life in heaven for us but by giving us victory at the physical level over attacks of the enemy.

We have to do our part, by walking in the righteousness of the blood of Jesus. We must place the Lord God Almighty first in our lives and first in our decisions. When we do that, we experience great inner peace. There are no terrible struggles of indecision because we *know* that we are doing what God wants us to do. We cast our cares on God, knowing that He carries them easily. He sustains us, holds us up, and supports us.

As He led the Israelites in a pillar of cloud by day and a pillar of fire in the night, so He leads us every second of our lives, never abandoning us, always blazing the trail ahead of us. All we must do is to trust Him and to follow Him.

*Wonderful Father God, I cast my burdens on You. Thank You for holding me and sustaining especially when I feel discouraged. Sometimes the enemy whispers that I am not righteous and not worthy of receiving my healing. Help me to take those thoughts captive and rebuke them as lies from the devil. I am righteous, Father, through the blood of Your precious Son. I give You every worry, Lord, and I trust You with my life. Thank You for guiding me and for healing me. In the name of Your Son, Jesus Christ, I pray, Amen.*

†

# DAY 12
## STEP OUT IN FAITH

*And, behold, a woman, which was diseased with an issue of blood twelve years, came behind him, and touched the hem of his garment: For she said within herself, If I may but touch his garment, I shall be whole. But when Jesus turned him about, and when he saw her, he said, Daughter, be of good comfort; thy faith hath made thee whole. And the woman was made whole from that hour. (Matthew 9:20-22)*

The woman in this famous Biblical story was confined to her home with a serious disorder of continuous bleeding. According to the law of the day she was considered to be unclean, and she could not go out in public without warning people to let them move away so that they would not be contaminated by her. If she were caught violating this rule, she would be stoned to death.

Can you imagine her friends bursting in the door excitedly telling her of a man called Jesus who was going from town to town, healing all who came to Him? "The blind see and the lame walk and the deaf hear," they reported to her. Perhaps the first time she heard this or perhaps over a period of time, she developed the belief that she would be healed if she could reach Jesus.

Next she spoke her belief. "If I may but touch his garment, I shall be whole." Notice that she did not hope for partial relief but for total healing. This statement of belief was verbalized, spoken out loud.  Over and over again Scripture tells us that what we speak is critical to what we get.  "Thou shalt also decree a thing, and it shall be established unto thee." (Job 22:28).  "If ye say unto this mountain, Be thou removed, and be cast into the sea; it shall be done" (Matthew 21:21).

Next she went into action.  She found the place where Jesus was, pressed through the crowd, and focused only on Him.  As a result, she got what she sought – a total, complete, instantaneous healing.  Notice that Jesus told the woman that it was her faith that made her whole.

Immerse yourself in God's Word and strengthen your belief system.  Faith comes by hearing and hearing by the Word of God.  It is faith that enables you to step out of what may look like a safety zone (even though it is a death trap) and reach for Your Savior.  It is faith that leads you to the Messiah who smiles at you and says, "Daughter, thy faith hath made thee whole."


*Almighty God, I have heard the good news!  I banish all feelings of fear and don't allow any distractions to stop me as I press forward in faith.  I declare with joy and confidence that by His stripes I am healed!  With a grateful heart, in Jesus' name, I pray, Amen.*

✝

# DAY 13
## BELIEVE BEFORE YOU RECEIVE

*Jesus saith unto him, Thomas, because thou hast seen me, thou hast believed: blessed are they that have not seen, and yet have believed.   (John 20:29)*

Some people believe that Scripture is somehow different for us because we live in the twenty-first century.   They wonder if the healings of Jesus were just for two thousand years ago so that people would understand that Jesus was really divine.   Or maybe the healings were just part of a sign for that particular time.   Or maybe we should not expect them to be relevant for us two millennia later.

But what about Jesus' statement that "Verily, verily, I say unto you, He that believeth on me, the works that I do shall he do also; and greater works than these shall he do; because I go unto my Father" (John 14:12).   Are you a believer?   Then you are supposed to be doing even greater works than Jesus did because you have His help and the help of the Holy Spirit.

Let go of the idea that you are operating at a disadvantage by living now instead of during the days when Jesus walked on earth because the opposite is actually true. Not only did Jesus give you the Holy Spirit, but He also sits at the right hand of the Father to act as mediator for you.

You are the recipient of the finished work of the Cross. "It is finished," Jesus said. It is finished especially for *you*. You have a new covenant sealed in the spotless blood of the Lamb and your healing was purchased and completed. The healing power of God is flowing every minute of every day because of the victory of the Cross.

Thomas refused to believe until he saw the evidence. Jesus asks you not to make the same mistake. Believe before you receive and you will manifest your healing.

*Father God, there are times when my unbelief seems to overtake me, but I cast down those thoughts. Thomas refused to believe until he could see the evidence, but I stand in faith, Father, as Jesus told me to do. Jesus spoke a special blessing on me for believing without seeing and I receive that blessing gratefully. I choose to believe that my healing is done, no matter what symptoms I may see temporarily. I stand on Your Word, and I focus my spiritual eyes on Your truth that by His stripes I was healed and am healed. Thank You, Father; thank You. In the name of Your Son, Jesus Christ, my Savior and my Redeemer, I pray, Amen.*

✝

# DAY 14
## BE CAREFUL WHAT YOU SAY

*For verily I say unto you, That whosoever shall say unto this mountain, Be thou removed, and be thou cast into the sea; and shall not doubt in his heart, but shall believe that those things which he saith shall come to pass; he shall have whatsoever he saith.*

*Therefore I say unto you, What things soever ye desire, when ye pray, believe that ye receive them, and ye shall have them.* (Mark 11:23-24)

Decide whether you want your words to manifest just as you say them. For example, suppose you are experiencing migraine headaches, but you do not have any real understanding of the finished work of the Cross. Medical tests reveal nothing so you do not know what to do. One morning you pray, "God, please heal me of my migraines."

Thirty minutes later, you say to your spouse, "I wonder if God heard me. My headache's already getting worse, and I'll bet it'll be killing me before the day is out." You say the same thing to several colleagues at work and sure enough you have a terrible headache. Then you come home and pray again, "God, I really want to be healed of these migraines." And so it goes.

Day after day you pray the same prayer, and day after day you voice your statements of doom. You keep "telling it like it is," which really means that you keep describing the problem. This reveals an underlying lack of faith in the innermost places of your heart, and it is fertile ground for satan to keep you separated from God's benefits.

Imagine the difference if you were to pray instead "Father, Your Word says that by His stripes I was healed, so I thank You that whatever is causing these headaches in my body is totally healed. I thank You, Lord, that whatever is at the very root of the problem is totally removed. Pain, you have no place in my body and I command you to leave in the name of Jesus. Through the blood of Jesus I am made whole."

God values words. He creates with His Word, and He expects you to do the same. You must understand that the words you speak are seeds that you are planting. God tells you that *you can have what you say.*

It is often helpful if you learn about your body and how it works. As you understand the mechanisms of health, you learn what made it easy for the enemy to attack you and what is needed to bring your body functions back into proper balance and operation. Once you know that information, then speak with authority to your illness, and in the name of Jesus command every organ in your body to operate according to God's design and plan for it.

For example, suppose you have been diagnosed with osteoporosis, a condition that occurs when bones lose their minerals and normal density. You might pray something like this,

"In the name of Jesus, I command my bones and the organs of my body to return to their proper function. I command my digestive system to assimilate properly the calcium, magnesium, boron, and other minerals which I am supplying to my body. I command my parathyroid glands to regulate my calcium levels properly. I command the osteoblast cells to wake up and to build new bone cells to make my bones strong and healthy. I command my body pH to return to normal and my kidneys to function healthily."

Make your words specific and authoritative. Speak in faith and see everything that you are saying as happening just as you speak the words. Proclaim and appropriate what Jesus has given you through the shed blood of the Cross. Then receive the healing power of God, your healer.

*Almighty God, I repent for my unbelief. I make a choice to believe what the Word of God says, and I make a decision to say only what the Word says that I am. Father, I choose to renew my mind and banish doubt by focusing on Your wonderful Word and powerful promises. I speak to my body and command every cell to function according to Your holy plan and design. By the stripes of Your Son, Jesus Christ, I was healed and am healed. Thank You, Father; thank You. In Jesus' name, I pray, Amen.*

†

# DAY 15
## DON'T STAY AROUND UNBELIEF

*And he cometh to Bethsaida; and they bring a blind man unto him, and besought him to touch him.*

*And he took the blind man by the hand, and led him out of the town; and when he had spit on his eyes, and put his hands upon him, he asked him if he saw aught.  And he looked up, and said, I see men as trees, walking.*

*After that he put his hands again upon his eyes, and made him look up: and he was restored, and saw every man clearly.* (Mark 8:22-25)

Since it took two attempts before the blind man at Bethsaida was healed, was there some momentary problem with Jesus' healing ability?  Of course not.

So what happened here?  The clue is given in a very important detail – the fact that the man spent a lot of time in Bethsaida.  Remember Jesus' words in Matthew 11:21-22 when He said, "Woe unto thee, Bethsaida! ...  It shall be more tolerable for Tyre and Sidon at the day of judgment, than for you."  Bethsaida was filled with unbelief and, despite the mighty works being done there, the people did not receive and believe.

This was the reason that Jesus took extra time to lead the blind man *out of the town* before even attempting to heal him.  The healing was then done progressively, in two stages, as the man was able to receive it. God's best is for us to receive our healing immediately, but He meets us where we are. God just wants us well and is pleased when we receive our healing, whether gradually or instantly. Jesus did not stop until the man was able to see one-hundred-percent perfectly. Do not ever forget that we do not have a part-way healer. We have a complete healer who has paid the price *in full*!

Before parting, Jesus warned the man not to return to Bethsaida but to go to his own house. Why? He did not want him to lose his healing. Many people have received their healing but then lose it by associating with people who do not share their beliefs. At the first sign of an old symptom, someone says, "See, your sickness isn't really gone" and before you know it, doubt rises up, the enemy rushes in, and the person is no better than before.

Declare your faith in your one-hundred-percent healing Savior. Lift your voice in gratitude and praise and receive your healing.

*Dear God, forgive me for entertaining thoughts of unbelief and doubt. I will be careful to surround myself only with those friends and people who speak faith-filled words. I will avoid listening to a mixture of opinions and will stand firmly and consistently on Your Holy Word which proclaims that by His stripes I was healed. Thank You, Father, for my healing. Thank You. In Jesus' name, I pray, Amen.*

✝

# DAY 16
## ALL THINGS ARE POSSIBLE
## IF YOU BELIEVE

*And one of the multitude answered and said, Master, I have brought unto thee my son, which hath a dumb spirit; and wheresoever he taketh him, he teareth him: and he foameth, and gnasheth with his teeth, and pineth away: and I spake to thy disciples that they should cast him out; and they could not. ...*

*And they brought him unto him: and when he saw him, straightway the spirit tare him; and he fell on the ground, and wallowed foaming. And he asked his father, How long is it ago since this came unto him? And he said, Of a child. And ofttimes it hath cast him into the fire, and into the waters, to destroy him: but if thou canst do any thing, have compassion on us, and help us. Jesus said unto him, If thou canst believe, all things are possible to him that believeth.*

*And straightway the father of the child cried out, and said with tears, Lord, I believe; help thou mine unbelief. When Jesus saw that the people came running together, he rebuked the foul spirit, saying unto him, Thou dumb and deaf spirit, I charge thee, come out of him, and enter no more into him. And the spirit cried, and rent him sore, and came out of him: and he was as one dead; insomuch that many said, He is dead. But Jesus took him by the hand, and lifted him up; and he arose.* (Mark 9:17-18, 20-27)

A father, desperate for healing for his son, turns to Jesus for help after the disciples have failed. He utters words of complete doubt when he asks, "*If you can do anything*, have compassion on us." Not even "if you *will*" but "if you *can*." He is afraid that his son is beyond the help even of Jesus.

We are no longer in the position of having to wonder as this man did if Jesus "can" heal us. We have the assurance of the finished work of the Cross that He has already taken our infirmities and sicknesses on Himself and conquered them. It is done. It is finished.

Notice that Jesus' response is to exhort the man to have faith. "All things are possible to him who believes." Imagine the look of compassion and love that He gives this distraught father.

What if you find yourself thinking, "Lord, can You do anything?" Immediately take those doubts captive because they are lies from the enemy. Quickly counter them with God's truth. Speak out loud saying, "It is written that by His stripes I was healed and therefore I am healed." Stand on His Word and receive your healing.

*Father God, I know that everything is possible for him who believes. When the enemy comes with whispers of doubt, I will draw ever closer to You in trust and obedience. I stand firm on Your Holy Word and give You praise for healing me. In Jesus' name, I pray, Amen.*

✝

# DAY 17
## TRUST GOD AND FOLLOW HIM

*And it came to pass, when Pharaoh had let the people go, that God led them not through the way of the land of the Philistines, although that was near. ... But God led the people about, through the way of the wilderness of the Red sea. ...*

*And the Lord went before them by day in a pillar of a cloud, to lead them the way; and by night in a pillar of fire, to give them light; to go by day and night: He took not away the pillar of the cloud by day, nor the pillar of fire by night, from before the people.*

*And the Lord spake unto Moses, saying, Speak unto the children of Israel, that they turn and encamp before Pi-hahiroth, between Migdol and the sea.    (Exodus 13:17-18, 21-22. Exodus 14:1-2)*

Imagine that you are one of the tired, frightened group of Israelites.  You have been in captivity in Egypt and after a terrible sequence of events you have been allowed to leave that country.  You are fleeing for your life, being lead by Moses.  Ahead of you, you see a pillar of cloud in the day and a pillar of fire in the night, a visible indication of the presence of the Lord your God.

Moses has declared that you and all the other Israelites will follow the instructions of the Lord God Almighty exactly as they are given.  Once on the road, you feel nervous about this whole journey, but you press on. Eventually, however, you become very alarmed because God has led you into what appears to be a trap. You can see nothing but the sea in front of you, and you know that the Egyptians are close behind, racing to catch up and to kill you.

Just as the Israelites so many years ago, we, too, are called to trust the Lord our God. If your healing has not manifested itself immediately, it may be more gradual and take a path that does not look like the most obvious one to you. It may not be what would be the "normal" treatment. On the surface, it may look like a trap, literally a dead-end road.

Do not allow your fear and the fears of others to set your course of recovery. Go to God in prayer, both alone and with your health care advisors. Listen to His voice. And once you receive your guidance, trust God. He will not fail you. When you least expect it, the sea will part, and you will walk to safety and healing.


*Lord God Almighty, You are my leader and my deliverer. Teach me to follow You faithfully and to trust You with my life. You have already made provision for my healing and You know just exactly what I need to do. I will walk the path You want me to follow. Thank You for parting the sea for me, Father. Thank You for healing me. In the name of Your Son, Jesus Christ, I pray, Amen.*

✝

# DAY 18
## GOD KEEPS HIS PROMISES

*O give thanks unto the Lord; call upon his name: make known his deeds among the people. ...*

*He brought them forth also with silver and gold: and there was not one feeble person among their tribes. ...*

*And he brought forth his people with joy, and his chosen with gladness.    (Psalm 105:1, 37, 43)*

In Psalm 105 the psalmist recounts the promises that God made to Abraham and the events that occurred as God kept His promises.

He tells of the captivity of the Israelites in Egypt and of the way that God delivered His people. In this amazing account, the psalmist declares "and there was not one feeble person among their tribes." Do you realize how harsh the living conditions were for the Israelites during their years of slavery in Egypt? A large proportion of God's people had to be sick, weak, and malnourished after years and years of this terrible, brutal slavery. But the people were told to eat the Passover Lamb and consequently there was not one feeble person among all the tribes that made the exodus from Egypt. What an astounding miracle!

Not one feeble person. God brought them out with joy and gladness – and with health in their bodies. God's healing power is awesome. He has revealed it over and over and over again. We have only to believe and to walk with God in obedience to Him. In verse 8 of Psalm 105 we read, "He hath remembered his covenant for ever, the word which he commanded to a thousand generations." God never forgets His covenant. He never forgets His promises to us.

God's story is one of redemption for His children. Jesus sacrificed Himself and became the Passover Lamb for us, thus winning our redemption for us. We were given the completeness of salvation, healing, deliverance, being made whole. When Jesus came, He repeatedly healed the sick, and He said, "Thy faith hath made thee whole" (Luke 17:19).

Rejoice! Rejoice! Your sins and infirmities were taken to the Cross two thousand years ago by Jesus Christ. It is done. God wants you to go forth with joy and gladness. He wants you to be well. Thank Him for your healing and let His glorious love fill you with joy.

*O gracious Father, I rejoice that I can trust Your covenant with me. As You led the Israelites, lead me and I will follow. Help me to remember these events of long ago and to draw strength from them. I glory in Your holy name and sing to You my songs of praise and thanks. I am Your child, and I trust in You to bring me forth with joy and gladness. In the name of Christ Jesus, my Savior and my Redeemer, I pray, Amen.*

†

# DAY 19
## AN EXAMPLE OF GREAT FAITH

*... And a certain centurion's servant, who was dear unto him, was sick, and ready to die. And when he heard of Jesus, he sent unto him the elders of the Jews, beseeching him that he would come and heal his servant. And when they came to Jesus, they besought him instantly, saying, That he was worthy for whom he should do this: for he loveth our nation, and he hath built us a synagogue. Then Jesus went with them.*

*And when he was now not far from the house, the centurion sent friends to him, saying unto him, Lord, trouble not thyself: for I am not worthy that thou shouldest enter under my roof: wherefore neither thought I myself worthy to come unto thee: but say in a word, and my servant shall be healed. For I also am a man set under authority, having under me soldiers, and I say unto one, Go, and he goeth; and to another, Come, and he cometh; and to my servant, Do this, and he doeth it.*

*When Jesus heard these things, he marveled at him, and turned him about, and said unto the people that followed him, I say unto you, I have not found so great faith, no, not in Israel. And they that were sent, returning the house, found the servant whole that had been sick. (Luke 7:2-10)*

In the time of Jesus the Romans occupied Palestine, and the soldiers were generally brutal, causing much enmity between the Romans and the Jews. Luke gives an account of a Roman centurion who had been good to the Jewish people. He heard about Jesus and His ability to heal people so he diplomatically contacted Jesus by sending Jewish elders with a message asking for Jesus' help in healing his servant. Jesus left immediately to go to the centurion's house, but before He could get there, the centurion sent some of his friends out to intercept Jesus. In behalf of the centurion, they said to Him, "Just say the word that my servant be healed and I know it will be done. I believe your authority is absolute. So you don't even need to come into my house."

Here we read that "Jesus marveled at him." Why? Because the centurion's actions revealed two fundamental beliefs – first, that Jesus had the power and authority to heal his servant, and, second, that Jesus' power was not limited in space. The centurion trusted that all that was necessary was for Jesus to speak the word of healing and it would be done.

Examine your own heart. Do you have the centurion's kind of deep and total faith in the healing power of Jesus Christ? Stand on God's Word and the healing authority of Jesus. Know that Jesus, your resurrected Savior, has borne the stripes for you, saying "it is done." Receive your healing now through the shed blood of the Cross.

*Almighty God, thank You for strengthening me as I deepen my faith. I declare my belief in Your Son, and I stand on Your Word which says that by His stripes I was healed. Thank You for the sacrifice and the blood of the Cross. Thank You for my healing. In Jesus' name, I pray, Amen.*

✝

# DAY 20
# GOD'S WORD NOURISHES US

*For as the rain cometh down, and the snow from heaven, and returneth not thither, but watereth the earth, and maketh it bring forth and bud, that it may give seed to the sower, and bread to the eater: So shall my word be that goeth forth out of my mouth: it shall not return unto me void, but it shall accomplish that which I please, and it shall prosper in the thing whereto I sent it. (Isaiah 55:10-11)*

Here in Isaiah we are told that God gave us His Word for a purpose and He means for it to accomplish something. God creates with His Word, and He compares His Word to rain that replenishes the earth and nurtures seeds that have been planted. He tells us that His Word never returns empty, but that it always accomplishes what He desires and achieves the purpose for which He sent it.

Isn't it a beautiful picture to see the rain and the snow coming down from heaven, watering the earth, and making the flowers and plants bud and spring to life? That is what God wants His Word to do for us. We are to receive the Word of God, to flourish, and to come to life under it because it is through the Word that God makes His message of love and redemption very, very clear.

God wants us to live fully according to His original plan for us rather than just to exist and make it through another day. Jesus told us, "I am come that they might have life, and that they might have it more abundantly" (John 10:10).

Allow God's Word to bloom in your heart. Set aside time every day to read His Word and to meditate on it. Hide it deep in your heart. Plant each of God's healing words in every cell of your body to grow and produce the fruit of recovery that God has ordained through His Word. Enjoy the same abundance of life that was present in the Garden of Eden – love, joy, peace, and constant communion with Father God.

God repeatedly tells us that His Word has power and authority. His Word is divine truth, and it can change your life if you will believe and have faith. It is written that Jehovah is the God who heals you. "Bud and flourish" according to His purpose.


*Almighty God, thank You for Your Word, the Holy Scripture, which never returns void to You. It instructs me, uplifts me, comforts me. No matter what my situation, Your Word is literally at my fingertips at every moment of the day and night. All I have to do is to read it, believe it, and act on it. Work Your purpose for my life in me, Father. Let Your Word sow seeds in me that will bud and flourish just as You intended. In Jesus' name, I pray, Amen.*

†

# Day 21
## Look Beyond the Appearance

*But the Lord said to Samuel, Look not on his appearance or at the height of his stature, for I have rejected him. For the Lord sees not as man sees; for man looks on the outward appearance, but the Lord looks on the heart.* (1 Samuel 16:7 Amplified Bible)

Samuel made a judgment about someone based on his appearance, and God reprimanded him for doing so. God told Samuel that He looks beyond a person's appearance and sees into the person's heart and soul. In fact, God looks beyond the appearance of all things to see the heart of each matter. This is particularly important for us to remember with issues of health.

Sometimes we manifest serious diseases: cancer, heart disease, diabetes, lupus. The list goes on and on. All of them exist. There may be legitimate medical treatments for many of them based on information provided from our three-dimensional world. But how does God see these illnesses? Does He focus on the appearance? Or does He see beyond to the heart of the matter?

Satan loves to get us diverted by the appearance of our illness, by our symptoms, and by the logic of what we define as reality. This is a very effective method to separate us from God's will. By tempting us to focus on disease "facts," he makes us forget the fact that the members of the early church (who were ordinary people like us) healed people regularly in spite of the appearance of terrible diseases.

You must decide which reality to trust and which reality to live. God asks you to see His reality. God asks you to look beyond the appearance of your disease. Acknowledge your symptoms as appearance only. See yourself as God sees you – whole and healthy. Now "call those things which be not as though they were" (Romans 4:17). Remember that you are looking at yourself the way that God looks at you through the blood of Jesus and the completed work of the Cross. Enforce the Word and command every cell in your body to function according to God's design and intent.

Repeat God's Word daily, hourly, or even minute by minute if necessary. Read God's Holy Word, believe, and trust.

*O, God, I choose Your divine will as my reality. No longer will I look at my body and be tempted to allow the appearance of disease to overwhelm me. I choose to see myself whole and well and to call myself completely healthy as You have instructed me to do. Father, I proclaim Your truth that You are the God who heals me and that by the stripes of Jesus I am healed. I rejoice in the completed work of the Cross and I receive my healing with love and gratitude. In Jesus' name, I pray, Amen.*

✝

# DAY 22
# POWER, LOVE, AND A SOUND MIND

*For God hath not given us the spirit of fear; but of power, and of love, and of a sound mind.* (2 Timothy 1:7)

God does not want us to be fearful. Repeatedly, He proclaims in His Word, "Fear not." Jesus' birth was heralded with the glorious announcement, "Fear not: for, behold, I bring you good tidings of great joy!" (Luke 2:10). Paul delivers the same message to us again in 2 Timothy.

Fear is the tool of the evil one. It keeps us victimized by illness and by people's actions, and it makes us weak. Fear separates us from God and keeps us from accepting God's true gifts.

What does God give us? Power! Not power over people to control them, but power to transform ourselves. Power to fulfill God's purpose in our lives. Power to spread God's Word to others. Power to overcome obstacles in our path. Jesus told us He brought us power ("dunamis") over all the power of the enemy, including sickness and disease.

God also gives us love which is the core of our Heavenly Father's essence. Jesus kept telling us, "God loves you! Love God and worship Him. As God loves you, love others. And as God loves you, love yourself. Love your neighbor *as yourself.*" When we connect to God's love and allow it to flow within our souls and bodies, we are healed. Love is the most powerful force in existence. It is infinitely stronger than sickness.

Lastly, God gives us a sound mind, which is sometimes translated as "self-control" or "self-discipline." These are our tools to do what we need to do. God always requires that we take action. We have to make the decisions to eat foods that are healthy for us, to get enough rest, to make time to play and laugh, and to walk, dance, or exercise.

All of this takes self-control and self-discipline. It is up to us to be willing to resist the temptations of the evil one and to align ourselves with God by following His guidelines for healthy living.

*Father God, thank You for giving me power, love, self-discipline, self-control, and a sound mind. I accept these gifts to help me fulfill Your purpose for my life. I take authority over the spirit of fear, and I renew my mind by meditating on Your holy Word. I choose to exercise self-control by doing those things which I know are healthy and avoiding those things which contribute to my illness. I speak to my body and I command every cell to function perfectly according to Your divine plan. Thank You, Father, for loving me and holding me in Your protective arms. In the name of Your Son, Jesus Christ, I pray, Amen.*

†

# DAY 23
## HAVE FAITH AND DON'T DOUBT

*Jesus answered and said unto them, Verily I say unto you, If ye have faith, and doubt not, ye shall not only do this which is done to the fig tree, but also if ye shall say unto this mountain, Be thou removed, and be thou cast into the sea; it shall be done. And all things, whatsoever ye shall ask in prayer, believing, ye shall receive. (Matthew 21:21-22)*

Jesus constantly stresses the importance of belief. He tells us that faith is the foundation of everything. Faith without doubting. Faith without unbelief.

Have you noticed how people have a way of having faith in God up to a point? Then they are controlled by their doubt and unbelief that God stands behind His Word and always performs it. People let their belief in the world around them take over and buy into what "facts" appear to be. They succumb to doubt that faith really can overcome everything.

Take a look at the story in Matthew 21. Jesus went to a fig tree which should have had fruit on it. He found it bare and told it that it would never bear again. Verse 19 tells us that at the word of Jesus, the tree "presently ... withered away." His disciples were amazed! Jesus responded to their shock by telling them that if they had faith and did not doubt, they could not only command fig trees to die but also they could tell a mountain to be cast into the sea.

61

Do you hear Jesus telling this to you today? He says to you that, if you follow His example, you can do not only what He does but also even "greater works" (John 14:12). Be careful not to be deceived by the evil one into believing that these words of Jesus applied to some special gift that was given only to the twelve disciples.

When you seek manifestation of your healing, know that it is the will of God that you be well. Believe. Remove all doubt from your mind because it will hinder you from receiving what God has already paid the price to give you. Renew your mind and banish every deceptive thought from the enemy.

Let your faith be strong as you stand in the presence of Jehovah-Rapha. Speak the Word, not hoping that you *will* receive your healing, but knowing that you have *already* received it. Proclaim in faith "It is written, by His stripes I was and am healed."

*Almighty God, Your Son, Jesus Christ, is Your perfect example. He tells me to believe with all my heart and soul. He tells me to have faith and not to doubt. Sometimes my medical reports seem discouraging but when I am tempted to see them as the only reality, help me to remember that Your report is a higher report and the only true report. I say to the mountain of my illness, "Leave my body," and I stand on Your Word that I am healed. In the name of Your Son, Jesus Christ, my Redeemer, I pray, Amen.*

†

# DAY 24
# GOD IS OUR DELIVERER

*He delivereth and rescueth, and he worketh signs and wonders in heaven and in earth, who hath delivered Daniel from the power of the lions.* (Daniel 6:27)

Taken captive by the Babylonians, Daniel came to be held in high esteem by several kings of that nation. King Belshazzar described Daniel this way: "I have even heard of thee, that the spirit of the gods [Spirit of God] is in thee, and that light and understanding and excellent wisdom is found in thee" (Daniel 5:14).

After Belshazzar was killed, Darius became the new king. Many of the people under King Darius were jealous of Daniel and tricked Darius into making a law forbidding any person from praying to anyone except the king for thirty days. Despite the new law, Daniel opened his windows, got down on his knees, and prayed to Jehovah three times a day just as he had always done. He was then brought before the king, who was forced to uphold his new law.

Daniel was taken to a den of lions, and a stone was laid against the mouth of the cave. The king was so upset that he did not get any sleep that night. The next morning he raced to the lion's den. Standing outside, he called, "Daniel, did your God deliver you from the lions?"

THE POWER OF GOD'S WORD FOR RECEIVING HEALING

To his relief, Daniel answered from within the den, "Yes! My God sent his angel and shut the lions' mouths so they didn't hurt me" (Daniel 6:20, 22). And Daniel was released.

Daniel was in a tight spot in the lions' den. If you feel sick, you are in a tight spot, too. The lions sought to devour Daniel, and the enemy seeks to devour your body and your strength. Daniel had to stand in faith, knowing that God was going to save him somehow. We have a major advantage over Daniel because we know that our enemy has already been defeated by our Lord Jesus Christ. We can boldly proclaim, "It is written that by His stripes I was healed so I certainly am healed!"

Our God is a Savior and Deliverer, who always keeps His Word. Just as He saved Daniel from the hungry lions, He has already sent His Word to heal you. Rejoice in your deliverance and recovery.

*Almighty Lord, how grateful I am for this wonderful story of Daniel which gives me an example of faith and trust in the most difficult circumstance. Like Daniel, I am standing, Father God. You do indeed work signs and wonders. Thank You for rescuing, delivering, and healing me. In the name of Your Son, Jesus Christ, my Redeemer, I pray, Amen.*

†

# Day 25
## Nothing Is Too Hard For God

*Ah Lord God! behold, thou hast made the heaven and the earth by thy great power and stretched out arm, and there is nothing too hard for thee. ...*

*Behold, I am the Lord, the God of all flesh: is there any thing too hard for me?*    (Jeremiah 32:17, 27)

Nothing is too hard for God, the great I AM. Nothing. Just by stretching out His arm and speaking the Word, God created the heavens and the earth. He is mighty and awesome, and yet He knows your name and He cares about you personally. You. Right here. Right now.

"Behold, I am the Lord, the God of all flesh: is there anything too hard for me?" What is God saying? He tells you that He is the God of all flesh. He created your flesh, and He designed your body. He created the pattern for each cell to function perfectly, and then He breathed life into each one.

Your flesh belongs to Him, and it is special and important because it was designed as the temple of the Holy Spirit. If you abuse your temple, you show disrespect for the Holy Spirit. If you succumb to temptations of the evil one, you set up an environment where disease can grow and flourish.

No matter what circumstances you find yourself in, there is nothing too difficult for God. If the prophet Jeremiah could proclaim this truth when the Messiah was still a promise to come, how much more can we shout our answer that nothing, nothing, nothing is too hard for God because we walk in the fulfillment of victory.

No matter how the evil one has affected your body, God is stronger and more powerful, and nothing is too hard for Him because He has overcome it all through the blood of Jesus. If disease has taken hold, it is not too hard for God to restore you. If an accident has injured you, it is not too hard for God to repair you.

God wants you to answer the question that He asks. "Is anything too hard for me?" What do you *really* believe?

*Dear God, You ask me a question: "Is anything too hard for me?" In the past I have had doubts and unbelief. But beginning right now, I choose to answer You by saying, "No, Father, nothing is too hard for You. Absolutely nothing." I rejoice that You sent Your Word and healed me. I rejoice that by the stripes of Your Son, Jesus Christ, I am healed. I rejoice that Jesus took my infirmities and bore my sicknesses. I rejoice that it is done. It is all done and all I have to do is to receive it. In Jesus' name, I pray, Amen.*

†

# Day 26
## Ask In Jesus' Name

*And whatsoever ye shall ask in my name, that will I do, that the Father may be glorified in the Son.*

*If ye shall ask any thing in my name, I will do it.* (John 14:13-14)

Once again, we are told to ask and it will be done as we request. Ask anything, Jesus says. But ask it in My name, He cautions us. Why in His name? Because Jesus won the victory for us and holds all power in heaven and on earth. When we ask in the name of Jesus, we are asking as a representative and as a follower of Jesus. Therefore, our asking has to be in line with the way Jesus would ask.

What does this mean? It means we must ask believing. And we must believe not only that God can do what we ask but that God wants to do what we ask. Jesus was always in agreement with God's will. He never asked God for something that He knew to be outside of God's will.

Jesus forgave people's sins and he healed all who received Him. He did not turn some away because God did not want a particular person to be forgiven or a particular person to be healed. Jesus knew that God wanted them *all* forgiven and God wanted them *all* healed.

God was glorified because His Son faithfully performed the works of the Father. And God is glorified when each of us acts as a vessel for Jesus to continue to do the works of the Father. The Amplified Bible reads, "And I will do [I Myself will grant] whatever you ask in my name [as presenting all that I AM], so that the Father may be glorified and extolled in (through) the Son."

Do not let satan talk you into believing God is glorified by your diseases. Instead, listen carefully to the words of Jesus. God is glorified when we choose to walk with Him and when we choose to follow His Son, Jesus Christ, by carrying on His work and keeping His commands.

Enforce God's Word and declare it with confidence and authority. Know deep in your heart that God's Word never returns to Him void. Trust and believe. Then let God's glory shine through to all who meet you.

*Lord God Almighty, I praise You, worship You, and glorify Your holy name. Your Word says that by the stripes of Jesus I am healed. Your Word says that Your Son took all my infirmities and sicknesses. I receive my healing, Father, in the name of Your Son, and I call forth the full manifestation of this healing. I stand in faith, Father, that it is done. In the name of the Jesus Christ, I pray, Amen.*

✝

# DAY 27
# THE BATTLE IS THE LORD'S

*Then said David to the Philistine, Thou comest to me with a sword, and with a spear, and with a shield: but I come to thee in the name of the Lord of hosts, the God of the armies of Israel, whom thou hast defied. ...*

*And all this assembly shall know that the Lord saveth not with sword and spear: for the battle is the Lord's, and he will give you into our hands.* (1 Samuel 17:45, 47)

When illness looms above us, it can seem as big and as mighty as Goliath looked to the Israelites. Read the entire story of David and Goliath in 1 Samuel 17. A nine-foot-tall giant stomps up and down, hurling insults and challenges to the Israelites. "Come on, I dare you. Send over your best man to try to kill me. If you win, we Philistines will be your subjects. If you lose, then you must be our subjects."

What was the response of the Israelites? Fear. Then young David comes in from tending his father's sheep and says, "Hey, what's this guy doing? Somebody needs to stop him." One of his brothers calls him conceited and tries to make him be quiet. However, David goes to Saul and offers to fight Goliath. After trying on some heavy armor, he takes it off and picks up five smooth stones. He goes before Goliath, tells him that "the battle is the Lord's," and then he kills the giant.

There are many lessons we can learn from this story. When we are hit with bad news from the doctor, the illness that has been diagnosed may seem as big as Goliath. The evil one wants to claim us, and he uses disease as his mighty giant.

But David did not see himself as small. He purposely remembered times in the past when he had been attacked by a lion and a bear. He specifically recalled the way that God had delivered him and brought him victory. He was focused on His faith in God and all He could see were the promises of God to defend him.

We have far better promises than David. We have the finished work of the Cross. We know that our Redeemer has come, has defeated the enemy, and reigns victorious. And everything that Jesus won, He gave to us. Healing is ours! Hallelujah! It is shouting time!

*Father God, thank You for the example of David who never saw himself small or helpless or defeated. I face my own Goliath – this health condition that wants dominance over me. I thank You for the sacrifice of Your Son, Jesus Christ, who has defeated the enemy and who gave me authority over all of satan's power. In the name of Jesus, I take that authority and bind every spirit of infirmity that has come against me. I declare that by the stripes of Jesus I am healed. Hallelujah! The victory is mine. Thank You, Father. Thank You. In Jesus' mighty name, I pray, Amen.*

✝

# Day 28
## God Is Never Weary

*Hast thou not known? hast thou not heard, that the everlasting God, the Lord, the Creator of the ends of the earth, fainteth not, neither is weary? there is no searching of his understanding.*

*He giveth power to the faint; and to them that have no might he increaseth strength.    (Isaiah 40:28-29)*

Do you not know?  Have you not heard?  Our Creator is the everlasting God!  How glorious!  Nothing – absolutely nothing – is beyond the power of God.

Often when we feel ill, we feel tired, tired, tired. Weariness attacks us down to our very bones.  Every chore looms like a giant hurdle and every task seems like a heavy burden.  At these moments turn your face to the Almighty God, your Creator and His Son, the Lord Jesus Christ.  Fill your heart with this Scripture that declares that Father God gives power to the faint. Jesus won that power for you when He defeated satan and all the forces of evil.  Father God doesn't grow tired or weary.  Not ever.  And He has released this power in an everlasting flow of divine love.

Set your eyes on your Risen Lord.  He stands in total victory and He pours out that strength on you.  Receive it. And say thank you.

The Word says we are to cast all our care upon Him, for He cares for us (1 Peter 5:7).  So name any cares you are carrying, wrap them in a bundle, and give them to Jesus. Only after you do this are you ready to rest unencumbered by burdens that hinder the healing of your soul, mind, and body.

Jesus told us to call Father God, "Abba." Abba is a term a child would use, similar to saying, "Daddy!" So envision the loving arms of Father God gathering you up just as a tender parent embraces a hurt and weary child. Sink into God's lap. Snuggle against His strong shoulder. Feel the divine healing power of God as you lean fully on Him.

Now feel His love and grace penetrate deep within you and flow into every cell in your body. Smile and rest in the Lord.

*Loving Father, You are the everlasting God. You are my Creator and the Creator of the ends of the earth. I give You my weakness and receive Your power and strength. Thank You for being with me, comforting me, enfolding Your loving arms around me, and holding me close to You. I rest in Your power and Your love. Thank You for renewing, restoring, and transforming every cell in my body. Help me to fulfill Your mission and Your purpose for me. With grateful thanks I pray in the name of Your Son, Jesus Christ, my Savior and my Redeemer, Amen.*

✝

# Day 29
# God Wants You Well

*O Lord my God, I cried unto thee, and thou hast healed me.*

*O Lord, thou hast brought up my soul from the grave: thou hast kept me alive, that I should not go down to the pit. (Psalm 30:2-3)*

And it came to pass, that when Jesus had finished these sayings, he departed from Galilee, and came into the coasts of Judaea beyond Jordan; And great multitudes followed him; and he healed them there.   (Matthew 19:1-2)

God's Word is filled with acts of healing.  From the Psalmist in the Old Testament who declares "You have healed me" to the healing ministry of Jesus in the New Testament, we are given account after account of God's healing power.

Take heart that God wants you to be well.  Where His will is worked perfectly – in heaven and in the life and ministry of His Son, Jesus Christ – there is no illness. Accept that into your consciousness at every level and dimension of your being.

Eliminate requests in your prayers such as "if it be Your will, please heal me."  Stand on God's Word and pray instead, "I receive Your healing, Jehovah-Rapha.  Let Your will be done on earth and in my life and in my body as it is in heaven."

Speak to every imbalance in your body and command each organ to function perfectly. Call every cell healthy, vital, and alive with divine healing power. For example, in the name of Jesus command the cells of your pancreas to secrete proper amounts of insulin and command the cells of your skeletal system to build healthy, strong bones. Enforce the Word of God on all the organs and cells of your body.

Listen for God's instruction about the ways that you are to participate in your healing, whether it be to undergo certain treatment or to use certain healing methods. Always be obedient to God's voice. Above all, give God all the glory for your healing. Rejoice, because by His stripes it has been done and you are healed.

*Father God, I cried to You, and You have healed me. You have brought up my soul from the grave. You have kept me alive so that I didn't go down into the pit. I joyfully proclaim my healing, and I rest in Your power and grace. Thank You for sending Your Son to carry my sins to the Cross and to bear all my infirmities. Thank You for all Your blessings, Father, and help me to be a faithful witness to Your great glory and mercy. In the name of Your Son, Jesus Christ, my Savior and my Redeemer, I pray, Amen.*

✝

# Day 30
## Stay On God's Path

*Show me thy ways, O Lord; teach me thy paths.*

*Lead me in thy truth, and teach me: for thou art the God of my salvation; on thee do I wait all the day.* (Psalm 25:4-5)

How easy it is to get off God's path. This is especially true when we are making decisions about our health. Even when we are clear about God's guidance, temptations abound to keep us from making healthy choices for our lives. We must remember "thou art the God of my salvation; on thee do I wait all the day." That means every moment of every day. No matter what.

As hard as it is to do what we need to do for our health when we know what the right thing is, it is harder still to find God's path when we are in doubt. Most health problems can be handled in several different ways. How do we know which is the path God wants us to take? Which is the particular way that God wants for us?

Often we are given very firm medical opinions that demand a certain path for treatment. To consider doing something different may feel very frightening. Usually, too, our family and friends have definite opinions about what we should do, and to fail to comply with their wishes is unsettling. Remember, the voice of fear often drowns out the voice of God so we must take our authority over such thoughts immediately.

Retreat into the heart of this psalm. "Show me *Your* ways, O Lord. Teach me *Your* paths." The opinions of others are important and it is right to give them prayerful consideration. However, your ultimate, final authority is the Almighty God. Quieten your mind. Tell your intellectual self to be quiet and put aside all assumptions.

As you attune your spiritual ears to the Holy Spirit, be still and listen for guidance. If you don't "hear" anything, then tell God you need help hearing Him. Ask Him to "speak up" and to make His pathway clearly known to you.

*Almighty God, I need Your help. I see lying symptoms, and I feel in my body how my lack of health affects me. Everyone around me seems to know what I should do. And most of them seem so sure of themselves. I come to You, Father, because You are the Great Physician. I stand on Your Holy Word, and I look beyond the appearance of these symptoms to Your truth. Let me hear Your voice clearly. Teach me to relax so that I can listen well. Send me Your guidance in the form I can hear it best. I know that by the stripes of Jesus I am healed and I am standing on Your Word, Father, until my healing in manifested. In Jesus' name, I pray, Amen.*

✝

# Day 31
# Let Go Of Your Fears

*Peace I leave with you, my peace I give unto you: not as the world giveth, give I unto you. Let not your heart be troubled, neither let it be afraid.* (John 14:27)

How often the message of God's Word tells us not to be afraid. Fear doesn't come from God. Fear is the work of the devil, and it separates us from God because love and fear can't operate simultaneously.

God is perfect love. Jesus, as part of the holy Trinity of Father, Son, and Holy Spirit, is also perfect love. In Him there was and is no room for fear. Whether confronted with satan, bad weather, multitudes of needy people, or a betrayer's kiss, Jesus remained at peace, centered in total love and peace.

Jesus calls you to Him and asks you to trust Him. "I give you my peace," He said. "Don't be afraid." The devil knows all our weaknesses, and he sends thoughts of fear to drive and torment us, including fears of being lonely, unloved, unworthy, poor, abused, rejected, and abandoned.

Deep in our hearts, a surprising number of us are afraid of being healthy. If we feel sick, we have an excuse to fail. If we feel sick, we have a reason to protect ourselves from a dangerous world. If we feel sick, we have "permission" to ask for kindness from others.

As long as we receive these hidden benefits from illness, our fears of being well are triggered, and the true desire of our heart is really to be sick. We must first cast the enemy and every spirit of fear out of us in order to create the proper environment for our healing. Choosing to live in faith instead of in fear would seem to be an easy choice, but it isn't. Jesus knows it takes courage to let go of our fears. He tells us He will help us and that He has His precious peace to give us.

We have to renew our minds and shift our focus. Confess the Word of God on a daily basis, and, if the fears try to return, take charge of your thoughts and banish the fears immediately. Accept the peace of Christ in your heart, and nestle under the wings of God, your healer.

*Almighty God, I am sorry for the times I have allowed fear to take root. I now choose to renew my mind with Your holy Word and replace every fear with faith and love. I won't let my heart be burdened with troubles, but I will cast them on Jesus as He told me to do. Thank You, Father, for enfolding me in Your loving, protective arms and surrounding me with Your strength, Your healing power, and the peace of Your Son, Jesus Christ, my Redeemer. I worship You, and I bless Your Holy name. In Jesus' name, I pray, Amen.*

✝

# Day 32
# Fear Is A Tool Of The Enemy

*There is no fear in love; but perfect love casteth out fear: because fear hath torment. He that feareth is not made perfect in love. (1 John 4:18)*

There is no fear in love. When we absorb God's love into the depths of our being, we will be at peace. We all seem to strive for this, but few seem to attain it. Why is this so?

Fear is one of the primary tools of satan. In fact, fear is one the devil's primary powers and principalities. The enemy takes every opportunity to remind us of our fears and tries to keep us focused on them. Eventually, he often even gets us to learn to love our fears or become addicted to them. Being fearful allows us to seek reassurance from our family and friends over and over again.

When we feel sick, our symptoms can change every day or every week, providing ample opportunity for giving us something new to be fearful about. Fear tries to suck us in and it keeps us just where satan wants us. We are no longer focused on God's Word. We are no longer sure of God's will. And we are no longer certain that the finished work of the Cross includes our healing.

However, to live in fear is a choice and to live in love is a choice. God allows us the free will to decide whether to choose love over fear. He extends His love to us every minute of every day and wants us to have it. His love is so boundless that He sent His Son for our salvation and healing.

Each time you feel fear about your health, replace it with a faith-seed from the Word of God. Quickly take captive every thought of fear, and renew your mind with victorious proclamations of Scripture.

Speak the Word, modifying Scripture to make it personally applicable to you. "I am the Lord that heals you" (Exodus 15:26). "By His stripes I was healed" (1 Peter 2:24). "Jesus Christ Himself took my infirmities and bare my sicknesses" (Matthew 8:17). "If I have faith as a grain of mustard seed, I shall say unto this mountain, 'Remove hence to yonder place,' and it shall remove; and nothing shall be impossible unto me" (Matthew 17:20). "He sent His Word and healed me" (Psalm 107:20).

Over and over again, speak the Word. Enforce it on every cell, tissue, gland, and organ of your body. Trust, believe, and accept God's love and healing with grateful thanks.


*Dear Heavenly Father, thank You for surrounding and enfolding me in the perfect safety of Your love. I break the bondage of fear and take every thought of worry and anxiety captive. I choose You, Your love, and Your healing. I choose to be well. In Jesus' name, I pray, Amen.*

## †

# DAY 33
# GOD RESCUES US

*And the multitude rose up together against them: and the magistrates rent off their clothes, and commanded to beat them.*

*And when they had laid many stripes upon them, they cast them into prison, charging the jailer to keep them safely:*

*Who, having received such a charge, thrust them into the inner prison, and made their feet fast in the stocks. And at midnight Paul and Silas prayed, and sang praises unto God: and the prisoners heard them.*

*And suddenly there was a great earthquake, so that the foundations of the prison were shaken: and immediately all the doors were opened, and every one's bands were loosed.* (Acts 16:22-26)

Over and over again we are given stories of the ways that God frees His people. Here we see Paul and Silas being brutally beaten and then thrown into prison unjustly. What was their response? To plot revenge or escape? To curse the people who had wronged them? No. What they did was to sing! There they were - wounded and hurting - and they were sitting in the jail cell singing hymns and praising God.

And, yes, they prayed. Stop for a minute and imagine what they might have been praying for. Healing? Deliverance? Forgiveness for those who had wronged them?

Guidance for what they were to do now? Perhaps all of these. In their case God answered dramatically and clearly. A great earthquake came, the prison walls were shaken and damaged, the prison doors flew open, and everybody's chains came loose. What a mighty God!

Now let's consider a situation that occurred many, many years before. Daniel, too, was wrongly imprisoned. He was sealed up in a den of lions. But look what happened. "My God hath sent his angel, and hath shut the lions' mouths, that they have not hurt me: forasmuch as before him innocency was found in me; and also before thee, O king, have I done no hurt [wrong]" (Daniel 6:22)

Know that no matter what your situation, you are the beloved child of the Lord God Almighty. Nothing is too hard for Him. There is no situation too hopeless for Him to change. We must accept our responsibility for doing our part in taking action according to the instructions of Jesus. We walk in the victory won for us through the shed blood on the Cross. With God's help we can overcome anything.

*Lord God Almighty, You are my strength and my salvation. No power is greater than You. Like Paul and Silas and Daniel, I pray to You and sing songs of thanksgiving in the face of my difficulties and tribulations. You are my great Redeemer and I thank You for my deliverance. In Jesus' name, I pray, Amen.*

†

# Day 34
# God Has Prepared Wonderful Things For You

*But as it is written, Eye hath not seen, nor ear heard, neither have entered into the heart of man, the things which God hath prepared for them that love him.* (1 Corinthians 2:9)

In your wildest imagination you can never picture all the wondrous things which your Heavenly Father wants to give you. One of the blessings that God wants His children to have is good health. When He created the Garden of Eden, He provided that Adam and Eve should be healthy, strong, and vital. There was no sickness or disease that could harm them.

Jesus came to show God's will for us, doing only those things that were according to God's plan and purpose. He healed everyone who came to Him to be made well. And when our time on this earth is done, we know that we will go to heaven, where God's perfect will always reigns. In the place of God's abode, there is no sickness or disease.

There is one requirement: that we love and obey God. Love is not simply an emotion that we feel. It consists of hundreds of thousands of actions minute by minute, based on our decisions and intent. Love is what you *do*. To love God means that you trust God with your entire being. To love God means that you ask Him for guidance in your life.

To love God means that you obey the instructions that you are given.

Most Christians think that they love, trust, and obey God at least most of the time. However, when they feel sick, the pattern is often to follow conventional methods of dealing with illness automatically. As long as the treatments are working or are not life-threatening, people rarely involve God in their recovery. It is only when surgery is pending or the treatments aren't working, that many go to God in prayer.

God doesn't want to be an afterthought. He wants to be your *first* consultation. To love God is to trust Him with your life and to be willing to seek His advice first. To love God is to be willing to obey His directives for your healing, regardless of what they might be. Stand fast in your love for Him. Stand fast in your trust that your eye has not seen and your ear has not heard nor has it entered into your heart the things which God has prepared for you.

*Father God, it is written that eye hath not seen nor ear heard, neither have entered into the heart of man, the things which You have prepared for those who love You. I love You, Lord. I love You. I believe Your Word and I trust You. I act on my faith, seek Your advice, and obey Your voice. Thank You, Father, for saving me, healing me, delivering me, prospering me, and making me whole. In the name of Your Son, Jesus Christ, I pray, Amen.*

✝

# DAY 35
# THE HOLY SPIRIT NEVER LEAVES YOU

*And I will ask the Father, and he will give you another Counselor to be with you forever – the Spirit of truth.     (John 14:16-17 New International Version)*

Jesus knew that His time in physical form on earth was short, so He told His disciples that He was asking the Father to send a counselor to be with them and with all His followers forever.  The Holy Spirit was present from the beginning, of course, as part of the Holy Trinity – God the Father, God the Son, and God the Holy Spirit.  But He was now being revealed to us in a new way and given to believers as a permanent, indwelling gift.

Who is the Holy Spirit?  He is the "Spirit of truth"   to show the way for us.  Like a compass which always turns to the north even in the darkest night, the Holy Spirit always points us to the capital-t Truth.

We live in the New Covenant and have the certainty that the Holy Spirit dwells inside every one of us who is born-again.  Make sure that you do not confess something that was true under the Old Covenant but that does not agree with the Word of God under the New Covenant.  Contrary to the numerous songs we hear in churches today that beseech the Holy Spirit to "come," Jesus makes it clear that the Holy Spirit never, ever leaves us.  To beg the Holy

Spirit to come when He never left reveals a lack of understanding of what Jesus has done for us. Only an unbeliever asks the Holy Spirit to come.

Many of the songs about the Holy Spirit are magnificent, but be very careful of the words that you sing. Lyrics to songs are powerful confessions. Watch for the ones based on Old Testament Scripture and Psalms which were written before Jesus had come and before Jesus sent the Holy Spirit to live within every believer always. Most people under the Old Covenant did not experience the presence of the Holy Spirit at all. And the ones who did rightly begged God not to take the Holy Spirit from them because they knew that His presence with them was only temporary.

When we are ill, we need the truth more than ever. It is easy to be deceived by the appearance of our illness and by the numerous opinions from the people around us. Therefore, ask the Holy Spirit to guide you whenever you have any decision to make. Receive daily revelation from your Counselor in gratitude as a vital part of your healing.

*Father God, thank You for the gift of the Holy Spirit who indwells me constantly as a born-again believer. Forgive me for the times I have forgotten to seek the advice of this Counselor in my daily life. I need His wisdom and His truth, and I express my gratitude that His guidance is always available to me. In Jesus' name, I pray, Amen.*

✝

# DAY 36
# GOD IS WORKING IN YOU

*Behold ye among the heathen [nations], and regard, and wonder marvelously: for I will work a work in your days, which ye will not believe, though it be told you.* (Habakkuk 1:5)

What an astounding statement! Habakkuk has been complaining to God that everything around him looked really bad. There was violence and destruction, and there did not seem to be any justice. He calls out to God saying, "O Lord, how long shall I cry, and thou wilt not hear!" (Habakkuk 1:2).

When we are dealing with illness and disease, how often are we tempted to succumb to the same feelings? Things within us don't seem to be looking good. There is a pain here and a pain there, a problem here, a problem there. One may seem to improve and two other problems pop up to take their place. The list goes on and on.

Like Habakkuk, we may call out, "O Lord, how long must I call for help? Are you there? Are you listening?" Deep inside, we may also be saying, "I feel afraid. I feel so afraid."

Look at God's response. "Behold and watch! Wonder marvelously! Be utterly amazed! Because I will work a work in your days that you would not believe, even if you were told." Everything comes down to faith, trust, belief. God wants us to be well.  We have to absorb that belief into our innermost being so that we can receive the mighty power that God has released.

"You wouldn't believe it even if I told you," God told Habakkuk.  But He did tell you!  He sent His Son, Jesus Christ, not only to tell you but to complete every thing that needed completing and to pay every debt that was due. Jesus bore your sins and your infirmities on the Cross.  It is finished.  It is done.  You no longer have to "wonder marvelously" because God has kept His Word and worked a work beyond your imagination.  He sent His own Son to die for you.  For you.  You are saved, healed, delivered, and made whole through the blood of the Savior.

*O, Lord God, forgive me for all the days that I have called for help in doubt and unbelief.  There have been times when I didn't think You were listening.  There have been times when I felt that what happened to my body seemed so unfair.  I know that those were times when I was listening to lies of the enemy instead of Your Holy Word.  I worship You, Father, and give grateful thanks for Your mighty works.  I do believe You, Father.  I do believe and I receive my healing now.  In the name of Your Son, Christ Jesus, my Redeemer, I pray, Amen.*

†

# DAY 37
# GOD IS FAITHFUL TO FINISH
# HIS GOOD WORK IN YOU

*Always in every prayer of mine for you all making request with joy, for your fellowship in the gospel from the first day until now;*

*Being confident of this very thing, that he which hath begun a good work in you will perform it until the day of Jesus Christ. (Philippians 1:4-6)*

Look at all the positive statements in this one sentence. What a lovely phrase: "making request with joy." No matter what situation we find ourselves in we need to pray with joy. Why? Because there is no situation that can happen to us that God has not already provided us the tools for victory. Not one.

"Fellowship in the gospel." How important it is that we stand on God's Word. And how important it is for us to fellowship in the Gospel with other believers who are walking in true discipleship. There is no mixture of belief in such a fellowship and no dilution of the power and authority that Jesus died to give us. The strength that comes from such agreement on the fundamental principles of the Word is essential to your spiritual growth and also to your emotional and physical health.

"Being confident of this very thing, that he which hath begun a good work in you will perform [complete] it until the day of Jesus Christ." Remember this and believe it when the road to your healing seems longer than you want it to be. Healing that comes instantaneously is God's best. But healing that is part of a longer process simply requires more persistence and more obedient action on our part.

What we have to remember is that God is always faithful to complete what He starts. He paid the full price for our healing two thousand years through the stripes and the blood of Jesus. It is done. It is finished. The Word says that by the stripes of Jesus Christ we were healed and the Word says that God's Word never returns void to Him. So we stand in faith. We persistently and faithfully stand until we see the manifestation of what we have asked.

And while we stand, we look to our Heavenly Father to be our primary consultant, our Great Physician. Every recommendation we receive from humans must be taken to Him for the final consultation. He will tell us exactly what to do, in minute detail, if we ask Him. He knows all the right choices for us and for our healing.

*Dear God, I am Your creation. You are always faithful to complete Your work in me and I praise and thank You for healing me. I am confident that You are faithful to complete every good work You have begun in me. In the name of Your Son, Jesus Christ, my Savior and Redeemer, I pray, Amen.*

✝

# DAY 38
# THE WORD OF THE LORD IS TRUTH

*... the son of the woman, the mistress of the house, fell sick; and his sickness was so sore, that there was no breath left in him. And she said unto Elijah, What have I to do with thee, O thou man of God? art thou come unto me to call my sin to remembrance, and to slay my son?*

*And he said unto her, Give me thy son. ... And he cried unto the Lord, and said, O Lord my God, hast thou also brought evil upon the widow with whom I sojourn, by slaying her son?*

*And he stretched himself upon the child three times, and cried unto the Lord, and said, O Lord my God, I pray thee, let this child's soul come into him again.*

*And the Lord heard the voice of Elijah; and the soul of the child came into him again, and he revived.*

*And Elijah took the child, and brought him down out of the chamber into the house, and delivered him unto his mother: and Elijah said, See, thy son liveth.*

*And the woman said to Elijah, Now by this I know that thou art a man of God, and that the word of the Lord in the mouth is truth.*
*(1 Kings 17:17-24)*

What is interesting about this story is to see who the woman and Elijah blame for the child's illness and death. The woman blames Elijah. "Art thou come unto me to call my sin to remembrance, and to slay my son?" She acknowledges that she has sinned but she does not take responsibility for it. Instead, she accuses Elijah.

Then Elijah cries out to God and blames Him. "O Lord my God, hast thou also brought evil upon the widow with whom I sojourn, by slaying her son?" We have gone from the woman's sin to "It's God's fault" in two quick steps.

Despite these accusations, what does God do? He raises the child from the dead.

God has established a system whereby we reap what is sown at both the physical and the spiritual levels. Yet when we experience the effects of our actions, we often do the same thing that Elijah and the widow did, which is to blame God rather than to take responsibility for the human factors that have led to the disease or problem.

Satan slips in to find our places of vulnerability, and he capitalizes on them, further encouraging us to sow unhealthy habits that have disastrous effects so long afterward that we do not even see the connection. Put the blame for illness where it belongs – on the evil one. And do not forget the conclusion the widow finally reached. She said, "the word of the Lord in the mouth is truth."

Make sure that the Word of the Lord is in your mouth. The Word is truth and the Word is liberty and the Word is healing. Declare the Word daily over your body and watch your healing manifest.

*Wonderful Jehovah-Rapha, I, too, am guilty of pointing the finger of blame at You when it is the evil one and often my own actions that have led to my illness. Forgive me, Father. I renew my mind, take responsibility for my actions, and speak Your Word over my life and my body. Thank You for healing me. In Jesus' name, I pray, Amen.*

✝

# Day 39
## Abide In Jesus

*If you live in Me [abide vitally united to Me] and My words remain in you and continue to live in your hearts, ask whatever you will, and it shall be done for you.* (John 15:7 Amplified Bible)

The Gospels are full of statements of the limitless power of God. This is one of them. Jesus has just been telling His disciples that He will not be with them much longer on earth. He is sharing with them precious truths that they must learn and absorb into their very being.

Over and over again Jesus has told His followers not to place limitations on God's love or God's power. Here He says, "Ask whatever you will, and it shall be done for you." Ask whatever you will. Jesus set the example and often His examples were in the realm of healing. He praised God for hearing Him and then called Lazarus to come forth from the dead. He told the lame to walk and the blind to see, and it was so.

Does Jesus give us any restrictions or conditions? Yes, there are two requirements in this Scripture. Notice the "if" part of the sentence. First, "if you live in Me." The Amplified Bible explains that this means to "abide vitally united" to Jesus. Think about what it means to live vitally united to Jesus. It means that your thoughts, your words, and your deeds will be in agreement with Christ. It means that you declare yourself to be a member of Jesus' family and that you are faithful to Him.

The second requirement is that Jesus' words "remain in you and continue to live in your heart." God repeatedly tells you of the importance of His Word. The Words of Jesus, the Son of God, are to fill you completely and to live in your heart. If they are alive in you, then they must be manifested in the things that you do and the things that you say.

Live vitally united with Jesus. Plant His Word deep in your heart. Live victoriously the life that Jesus died to purchase for you. Ask whatsoever you will and it will be done unto you according to the Word of Jesus.

*Dear God, I declare my faith in You and in Your Son, Jesus Christ. Thank You for coming into my heart, Lord Jesus. I seek to live united with You in every aspect of my life. I join with You at every level and dimension of my being. Thank You for forgiving my sins, cleansing me, and healing my body. I cherish Your Holy Word and commit myself to reading it, studying it, and meditating on it daily. As I live united with You, guide me and show me how I can be a better disciple and a better witness for You. With grateful thanks, in Jesus' name, I pray, Amen.*

†

# DAY 40
## SPEAK TO YOUR BODY

*The hand of the Lord was upon me, and carried me out in the spirit of the Lord, and set me down in the midst of the valley which was full of bones. ... And he said unto me, Son of man, can these bones live? And I answered, O Lord God, thou knowest. Again he said unto me, Prophesy upon these bones, and say unto them, O ye dry bones, hear the word of the Lord.*

*Thus saith the Lord God unto these bones; Behold, I will cause breath to enter into you, and ye shall live: And I will lay sinews upon you, and will bring up flesh upon you, and cover you with skin, and put breath in you, and ye shall live; and ye shall know that I am the Lord. ... behold a shaking, and the bones came together, bone to his bone. And when I beheld, lo, the sinews, and the flesh came up upon them, and the skin covered them above: but there was no breath in them.*

*Then said he unto me, Prophesy unto the wind, prophesy, son of man, and say to the wind, Thus saith the Lord God; Come from the four winds, O breath, and breathe upon these slain, that they may live. So I prophesied as he commanded me, and the breath came into them, and they lived, and stood up upon their feet, an exceeding great army.*   (Ezekiel 37:1, 3-10)

There are sometimes moments when we are tempted to allow ourselves to despair that we will be healed. At those times read this passage from God's Word. In this vision

Ezekiel is in the midst of a valley of dried up bones and God challenges him with a question, "Can these bones live?" Ezekiel knew that God had the power to transform anything. The question in Ezekiel's mind was whether God willed it. So he replied, "O, Lord God, thou knowest."

Now watch what happens. God doesn't just reach down and put flesh on the bones. He uses Ezekiel as His instrument and works through him. "Now Ezekiel," God says. "You speak to these bones. You tell them I will put tendons and flesh on them and will breathe the breath of life into them." God does the work but Ezekiel has to speak God's truth.

We are not like Ezekiel who waited for God to breathe life into those bones. We have the glorious gift of the finished work of the Cross. It is done. It is completed. Yet like Ezekiel, we must speak the Word and enforce every gift of the atonement in our lives. We proclaim loudly and joyfully, "Jesus took my infirmities and bore my sicknesses. By His stripes I was healed and am healed." Hallelujah!

*Mighty Lord, I speak to my body in the name of Jesus and command every organ and cell to function normally. Like Ezekiel, I stand in wonder as You perform Your Word and restore me to health. Thank You, Father, for the breath of life and the shed blood of Jesus that paid every price and insures that I walk in victory all my days. In Jesus' name, I pray, Amen.*

†

# DAY 41
# THE VICTORY IS YOURS

*And when he was entered into a ship, his disciples followed him. And, behold, there arose a great tempest in the sea, insomuch that the ship was covered with the waves: but he was asleep.*

*And his disciples came to him, and awoke him, saying, Lord, save us: we perish.*

*And he saith unto them, Why are ye fearful, O ye of little faith? Then he arose, and rebuked the winds and the sea; and there was a great calm.   (Matthew 8:23-26)*

We can all relate to times in our lives when everything seems to be smooth sailing, and then suddenly, without warning, a furious storm comes up.  Usually illness comes upon us gradually day by day, step by step, as we make decisions that are not wise ones.  However, occasionally, the evil one unleashes his attack suddenly and without warning.  A car crashes into us or something else happens rapidly and swiftly.   One moment we were healthy and the next moment we are wounded or ill.

How do we respond at those times?   Unfortunately, sometimes some of us react in ways not so different from Jesus' disciples.  When the violent storm came up suddenly, they became terrified as the waves swept over the boat.  They were afraid for their lives and they yelled to Jesus to save them. Focused on the outcome they feared, they shouted, "Lord, save us; we perish."

And what was Jesus doing? He was sleeping through the storm. When He was wakened, He got up and chastised His disciples. "Why are you fearful? Where is your faith? You should have exercised your authority." But He then rebuked the wind and the sea, and restored calm in their lives.

When illness or injury happens to you, remember this story. Let Christ Jesus speak to you, saying, "Don't be fearful. Have faith! And take your authority!" Jesus is our victorious conqueror of anything and everything that the evil one can throw at us. Follow His example and rebuke whatever is attacking you. Stop wasting your energy on lamenting your problem and start enforcing God's power in your life and in your healing.

*Almighty God, keep me focused on You and Christ Jesus, who repeatedly showed me by His example that fear is not from You. Despite the storm around Him, He slept peacefully, resting in His faith in Your protective care. I hear Him speak to me through the Word telling me not to be afraid and to take my delegated authority over all attacks of the enemy. I choose now to immerse myself in the truth of Your Word because I know that faith comes by hearing and hearing by Your Holy Word. In the name of Your Son, Jesus Christ, my Savior and my Redeemer, I pray, Amen.*

✝

# Day 42
## Patience Is Endurance

*That ye be not slothful, but followers of them who through faith and patience inherit the promises.* (Hebrews 6:12)

Sometimes God's path for our healing takes only an instant. But at other times it is a slower process. We have to hold to our faith and be diligent in our efforts so that we will inherit what has been promised. We have already been redeemed, body, soul, and spirit, by Jesus Christ on the Cross. The promise is that the healing that has already been accomplished through Jesus Christ can be made manifest in our own body and life.

Having patience doesn't mean sitting around and waiting for God to "move." God already "moved" two thousand years ago. When Jesus said, "It is finished," He meant it. We are told that in order to inherit the promises we must not be slothful or lazy. Once again we are told that we must act. We have to be a doer of the Word.

We have to take authority over the attacks of the enemy according to Luke 10:19. We have to command every organ, gland, and cell to operate perfectly according to the stated will of Father God. We have to stop judging our recovery by signs of change in our symptoms. We have to refrain from looking at the appearance of things, such as whether our vision is blurred or our hands shake or our knee hurts.

To base your belief according to the appearance of your symptoms undermines your faith because your inner voice is really saying, "If my vision is still distorted, then I'm not healed." That is the voice of doubt. The father of lies wants to keep you focused on anything that can make you doubt the finished work of the Cross. He loves to keep you checking and double-checking for signs of improvement.

We are exhorted to keep standing – tough, stubborn, patient. "Wherefore take unto you the whole armour of God, that ye may be able to withstand in the evil day, and having done all, to stand" (Ephesians 6:13). There are certainly times when the devil throws up every obstacle he can find to hinder your progress. At these times instead of concentrating on your symptoms, keep your eyes on the Cross. Stand on the Word which says, "Himself took our infirmities, and bare our sicknesses" (Matthew 8:17).

Trust in God. Thank Him for healing you. And so it is.


*Father God, teach me to be steadfastly focused on Your Word and the finished work of the Cross. Help me not to be lazy, but to stand strong so that I may inherit every promise You have made. Let me be an example to others of the victory that Jesus won for me. And let me manifest health in my body and sow the seed of the Word to all I meet. In Jesus' name, I pray, Amen.*

†

# Day 43
# Trust God

*They that trust in the Lord shall be as mount Zion, which cannot be removed, but abideth for ever.   (Psalm 125:1)*

O, to have unshakable trust!  Trusting God "ought" to be the easiest thing in the world to do.  Often it's easy enough to say we trust.  But our thoughts and our actions bear the fingerprints of the lack of the trust we proclaim.

The enemy seeks to undermine our trust at every opportunity.  One excellent way to do this is by attacking our health and using emotions to separate us from relying on God.  If the medical news is bad, we may react in a myriad of ways.  Sometimes we get angry and wonder why God "let" it happen.  Sometimes we become depressed and surrender to despair.  Sometimes we panic and become overwhelmed at the scientific opinions which are presented to us as absolute fact.  Sometimes we sob with fear.  Other times we shut down our emotions and refuse to feel anything or confront our situation.

No matter what the challenge, we must trust God and not allow our emotions to rule us because they are part of our soulish realm.  The Word says that we are supposed to be led by the Holy Spirit who lives within us and directs our own spirit.  We have to be in a place of spiritual trust before we can hear the Holy Spirit clearly when He shows us the path we need to take. And it is because of our trust that we choose to follow through and hold to God's path in spite of people and events that would be obstacles to us.

Trust is the foundation of our relationship with God. When it comes to our health, the appearance of trust is easy. The reality of putting trust in God before putting trust in any human being (including family, friends, and medical personnel) is sometimes quite difficult. Trusting God does not mean that you disregard the opinions and advice of others, but it does mean that you allow God's guidance to determine the choices you make. Take a deep breath now and declare your faith in your Creator.

*Mighty Father, I choose to live in trust with every breath I take. There are times that I struggle, and I realize that I have wandered off the path You mean for me to walk. I take captive all thoughts of fear and doubt, and I choose to trust You, Father. Your Word says that You want only good for me and I trust You to guide me as I walk the path of recovery. Thank You for the supreme sacrifice of Jesus on the Cross to purchase my salvation, deliverance, and complete healing. I receive it now, Father. In the name of Your Son, Jesus Christ, my Savior and my Redeemer, I pray, Amen.*

†

# DAY 44
# PRESS IN TO THE LORD
# FOR YOUR HEALING

*And a woman having an issue of blood twelve years, which had spent all her living upon physicians, neither could be healed of any, came behind him, and touched the border of his garment: and immediately her issue of blood stanched.*

*And Jesus said, Who touched me? When all denied, Peter and they that were with him said, Master, the multitude throng thee and press thee, and sayest thou, Who touched me? And Jesus said, Somebody hath touched me: for I perceive that virtue is gone out of me.*

*And when the woman saw that she was not hid, she came trembling, and falling down before him, she declared unto him before all the people for what cause she had touched him, and how she was healed immediately. And he said unto her, Daughter, be of good comfort: thy faith hath made thee whole; go in peace. (Luke 8:43-48)*

We are taking a second look at the story of the woman with the issue of blood (see Day 12) because Luke gives us several details that were omitted by Matthew. The woman with an issue of blood had suffered for twelve long years, going from doctor to doctor for help. By the time the story is told, she had spent all her money on medical care, yet she was no better at all. She heard about Jesus and made up her mind that all that was necessary for her healing was simply to touch the hem of His robe. That level of faith makes an inspiring story by itself; however, there are other elements that make the woman's story even more powerful.

In Jesus' time it was illegal for women having "an issue of blood" to appear in public. For this woman to leave her house was exceedingly risky because the penalty was death by stoning. In spite of this, the woman dared to go out to seek the man she believed could heal her.

Once she got close to Him, she must have been shocked to discover that He was walking with Jarius, who was a ruler of the synagogue. This little detail found in verse 41 is critically important because here was the very man who had the authority to have her killed on the spot if he discovered her. Did she dare to take another step forward to reach Jesus?

Gather your own courage in dealing with your own sickness so that nothing keeps you from pressing in to reach your Savior and your healer. He has already paid the price for you and has taken the stripes to make you whole. Reach out in faith to Him.


*Almighty God, like the woman with the issue of blood, I have suffered with my health problem for a long time. The solutions that I have tried haven't brought the healing I seek. My answers are in You, Father, and in the finished work of the Cross, by which I was healed. I receive the manifestation of my healing now. In Jesus' name, I pray, Amen.*

†

# DAY 45
## REACH OUT AND GRAB YOUR HEALING

*When she had heard of Jesus, came in the press behind, and touched his garment. For she said, If I may touch but his clothes, I shall be whole.* (Mark 5:27-28)

*And when Jesus was come into Peter's house, he saw his wife's mother laid, and sick of a fever. And he touched her hand, and the fever left her: and she arose, and ministered unto them.* (Matthew 8:14-15)

*And when he was come into the house, the blind men came to him: and Jesus saith unto them, Believe ye that I am able to do this? They said unto him, Yea, Lord. Then touched he their eyes, saying, According to your faith be it unto you.* (Matthew 9:28-29)

*And one of them smote the servant of the high priest, and cut off his right ear. And Jesus answered and said, Suffer ye thus far. And he touched his ear, and healed him.* (Luke 22:50-51)

The Scriptures come alive in wonderful ways when we do a little study of the original Greek. Let's look at the word "touch" which appears in the Scriptures above. In English we think of a touch as light, gentle contact. Sometimes it can be so soft that a person hardly knows that he has been touched.

Yet the Greek word used in each of these verses means something very different. It means to grasp firmly, to hold tightly, to attach oneself to, to fasten to, and to touch. This is not a wimpy, anemic action, but instead it is forceful and meaningful. The woman with the issue of blood was risking her life by being out in public so when she finally got to Jesus, she reached out with determination and grabbed tightly to receive her healing.

It is just as interesting to see that when Jesus "touched" people to heal them, He was not giving them a gentle tap with His finger. Notice that He often grasped people firmly. He took Peter's mother-in-law firmly by the hand. And he grabbed hold of Malchus' head where Peter had cut off his ear.

Let's focus our intent and not be tentative as we reach out to receive our healing. We stand in confidence and boldness, knowing that God is our healer and that our victory has been won by the stripes of Jesus.

*Heavenly Father, I know that Jesus has borne my sicknesses on the Cross and that everything has been accomplished by the atonement and the brutal stripes that He took for me. I reach out now and grab hold of my healing. And I'm not letting go. In Jesus' name, I pray, Amen.*

✝

# DAY 46
# WE SHOULD DIE HEALTHY

*These wait all upon thee; that thou mayest give them their meat in due season. That thou givest them they gather: thou openest thine hand, they are filled with good. Thou hidest thy face, they are troubled: thou takest away their breath, they die, and return to their dust.* (Psalm 104:27-29)

In this psalm David speaks of death. "Thou takest away their breath, they die, and return to their dust." This depiction of death is interesting because it shows the way we are really supposed to die. The psalmist has just told us that God gives us food to nourish us and that He fills us with good things. Among those good things is a life lived in service to the Lord. God breathed in Adam the breath of life, and He does the same for each one of us. He wants us to fulfill the number of our days and then, when it is time, He will simply "take away our breath" and we will die.

We should live a long, healthy life in service to God and for His glory. There is no reason why we should die a long and agonizing death. That is part of satan's plan, not God's. Jesus plainly said He did only those things that were the will of God. He certainly would not have worked so hard and so consistently to heal people if it weren't God's will for us to be well.

What happens when God's plan is subverted by the evil one? We die early before our time. Take a look at every account in Scripture of someone being raised from the dead either in the Old Testament or the New Testament. It was never a person who had already fulfilled his years; it was always someone who had died prematurely. Satan delights in interfering with God's plans, but even where he succeeds in killing people early, God always brings those who are born-again to Himself for eternity.

If we live in partnership with God and accept responsibility for our health, we will take the actions we need to take for being well. We then affirm to God our desire to live and receive God's blessings, including good health.

When we have fulfilled our days and it is time to be welcomed to our heavenly home, we simply let God take back the breath of life and move us to the place Jesus has prepared for us, according to His Word and His promise.

*Lord God Almighty, I want to fulfill my days in this bodily temple in good health and in total service to You. When the time comes and I am very, very old, I look forward to Your taking my earthly breath as gently as You gave it and then to being with You in my heavenly home. In the name of Your Son, Jesus Christ, I pray, Amen.*

† 

# Day 47
# You Are An Overcomer Through Christ

*Behold, the hour cometh, yea, is now come, that ye shall be scattered, every man to his own, and shall leave me alone: and yet I am not alone, because the Father is with me.*

*These things I have spoken unto you, that in me ye might have peace. In the world ye shall have tribulation: but be of good cheer; I have overcome the world.* (John 16:32-33)

Jesus never promised that we wouldn't have trials and tribulations. In fact, He told us that we would. Not only that, He told us that we would have many tribulations particularly because we were following Him. In this passage of Scripture, Jesus has just told His disciples that He is soon to be killed and that the disciples will run away and hide. In other words, satan was going to target not only Jesus but also His followers.

But that isn't the real message Jesus wants to leave with them. He says, "I am telling you this not only so that you can understand what is happening but also so that you can see beyond the appearance of things. I want you to have peace in your heart. I already forgive you for deserting me. And you must understand that I have overcome the world. I have overcome everything that satan has ever done or that satan can ever do. I have overcome it *all*."

This was an important message because the arrest, trial, beating, torture by crucifixion, tyranny, rejection, and abuse that Jesus suffered were examples of the kinds of tribulations that the disciples and followers of Christ would experience later. The enemy would throw at them every attack possible. Yes, that might even include sickness and disease. However, illness was not an adversity that Jesus wanted to hinder the mission of His followers, so the disciples were given power by Jesus to heal all diseases in the name of Christ. They were taught by Jesus how to do this, and He expected them (Matthew 10:8) and us (Mark 16:18) to follow His instructions and commands.

No matter what happens to you, be of good courage! Jesus has overcome the world. We are to stay focused on Jesus because He is the source of our peace and our victory. Keep your eyes focused on Him, His love, and His promises. Do not let your gaze waver from Him.

*Almighty God, help me to keep my focus on You and to remember that Jesus has overcome the world and reigns triumphant. Father, I make a choice to be cheerful, courageous, and strong because I know that Jesus has purchased my healing with the stripes on His back. In Jesus' mighty name, I pray, Amen.*

✝

# DAY 48
## DO NOT WORRY

*So do not worry or be anxious about tomorrow, for tomorrow will have worries and anxieties of its own. Sufficient for each day is its own trouble.* (Matthew 6:34 Amplified Bible)

Worry is actually the voice of the enemy whispering in your head, and it puts you in partnership with satan instead of with God. Once you begin worrying, there seems to be no end to it. What if this? What if that? Maybe this. Maybe that. Should I do this? Or should I do that?

Worry has many physical consequences. It drains you and depletes your energy. It puts a great strain on your immune system and, thus, interferes with your ability to fight infection and disease. It creates imbalance in your body down to the cellular level. When you feel sick, you are in a very vulnerable position, and it is all too easy to succumb to constant worrying. It is essential that you take control over your thoughts and stay grounded in your faith.

Because of the way our culture has developed, most of us have become very dependent on believing that modern medicine is the solution to all our health problems. But do not forget that there is a natural healing approach as well. Be willing to consider God's own remedies, which He spread over the planet in extraordinary profusion. Herbs, essential oils, and natural substances are part of God's great blanket of healing.

When you first notice a symptom, do not waste your energy by worrying about it. Take authority over it and command in the name of Jesus for that symptom to leave you. Then talk to God. If He wants you to do something other than to deal with your problem at the spiritual level, He will tell you. If you are told to seek a medical professional, do it. Or if you are told to go to the natural world for your healing, do it.

Never give in to worry. Jesus exhorts you to walk in faith and trust in Him. Speak the Word and receive your healing.

*Almighty God, I admit that I've allowed feelings of worry to occupy my mind even though Jesus told me not to be anxious. Therefore, I take authority right now over worry, anxiety, and stress, bringing every thought into captivity to the obedience of Christ. I choose instead to fill my mind with Your Word, Father, which says that "Himself took my illnesses and bore my sicknesses" and "By His stripes I am healed." Thank You, Father, for Your encouragement, Your truth, and Your healing. In the name of Your Son, Jesus Christ, I pray, Amen.*

†

# DAY 49
# JESUS HEALS EVERY DISEASE

*And when he had called unto him his twelve disciples, he gave them power against unclean spirits, to cast them out, and to heal all manner of sickness and all manner of disease. (Matthew 10:1)*

Once again we see the scene of Jesus passing on to His followers His authority over demonic spirits and over sickness and disease. They needed power over both these areas because there is usually a link between them. Notice that no sickness was beyond the power of healing by the disciples. Not a single one.

Why is the emphasis on deliverance and healing important? Because God is restoring His original plan for us. He has never stopped loving us, and He wants every one of His children to live as He intends. He wants us to live whole and complete standing before Him just as Adam did before he chose to know evil.

God never removes from us the right of free will. He always allows us to choose partnership with satan instead of with Him. But through the sacrifice of the body of Jesus Christ, God offered wholeness to us once again while we are still in physical form. Jesus tells us of that over and over again. "Your faith has made you whole," He said to one person after another.

Do not let satan keep you from being healed. Jesus gives us the authority to reclaim our bodies, and He gives us the authority to expel demons. Jesus bore not only our sins on the Cross but also our sicknesses. It is written! Hallelujah! How blessed we are!

Receive the healing of Christ this moment. Enforce the Word on every cell of your body. Remember that Jehovah-Rapha is the "God who quickeneth [gives life to] the dead, and calleth those things which be not as though they were" (Romans 4:17). Call yourself whole and receive your healing.

*Thank You, God, for healing me. I praise Your mighty name and glorify You for all the miracles You work in my life. I declare my willingness to follow Your Son, Jesus Christ, and to carry on His mission. I accept His call to be one of His disciples, and according to Your Holy Word, I know that He gives me power and authority over sickness just as He gave power and authority to His followers two thousand years ago. In His name, I command every organ, gland, tissue, and cell to function normally according to Your divine plan. I stand on the Word which says, "With His stripes I am healed." With grateful thanks in Jesus' name, I pray, Amen.*

†

# Day 50
# A Prayer For Boldness

*And now, Lord, behold their threatenings: and grant unto thy servants, that with all boldness they may speak thy word,*

*By stretching forth thine hand to heal; and that signs and wonders may be done by the name of thy holy child Jesus.*

*And when they had prayed, the place was shaken where they were assembled together; and they were all filled with the Holy Ghost, and they spake the word of God with boldness.* (Acts 4:29-31)

It is interesting that these verses are sometimes given the subtitle, "Apostles' Prayer for Boldness." When we feel sick, we can certainly use boldness to take hold of our healing that was won for us on the Cross.

What does the prayer contain? First, it acknowledges the supreme sovereignty of Jehovah, the mighty I AM. "Lord, thou art God, which hast made heaven, and earth, and the sea, and all that in them is" (Acts 4:24). Next, it quotes Holy Scripture from the Psalms of David and then speaks of those who conspired against Jesus. Last, it makes certain requests of God.

What do the believers ask for? Boldness to speak the Word that says that Father God stretches out His hand and heals. Here again we see the dual mission revealed – teaching the Word and healing the sick.

We are no different from the first believers. We have the same spiritual needs and the same physical needs. The evil one often tries to convince us that times are different now and that the signs and wonders that applied to the early church do not apply to us today. But Jesus is the same yesterday, today, and tomorrow. The Lord God Jehovah is the same God with the same will and the same power. We should pray the same prayer of boldness of the believers and expect the same results. Pray it right now.

*Almighty Father, I am a believer. I am a believer just like the believers who lived two thousand years ago, so I pray the prayer of believers, the prayer for boldness, as it is recorded in Your Holy Scripture: Lord, You are God. You made the heaven and the earth and the sea and everything in them. You spoke by the Holy Spirit through the mouth of your servant, our father David. Enable me, Father, to speak Your Word with great boldness as I witness Your stretching out Your hand to heal and to perform miraculous signs and wonders through the name of Your holy child Jesus. In Jesus' name, I pray, Amen.*

†

# DAY 51
## JESUS BRINGS YOU LIBERTY

*And he was teaching in one of the synagogues on the sabbath. And, behold, there was a woman which had a spirit of infirmity eighteen years, and was bowed together, and could in no wise lift up herself.*

*And when Jesus saw her, he called her to him, and said unto her, Woman, thou art loosed from thine infirmity. And he laid his hands on her: and immediately she was made straight, and glorified God. ...*

*... ought not this woman, being a daughter of Abraham, whom Satan hath bound, lo, these eighteen years, be loosed from this bond on the sabbath day?* (Luke 13:10-13, 16)

A woman had been crippled by a spirit of infirmity for eighteen long years. Jesus saw her and called her to Him. What did He do? He did what He was sent by the Father to do for all of us: He set her at liberty. "Woman," He said, "thou art loosed from thine infirmity."

Satan wants to bind all of us. We are his target, and he seeks to control us by making us weak and helpless. He binds us through finding our inner vulnerabilities and weaknesses and attacking us with spirits of anger, guilt, shame, fear, grief, loneliness, and infirmity. He convinces us to focus on our losses and to spend our days seeking revenge or crying with sorrow and regret.

He also binds us by misleading us and getting us to make unwise choices leading to actions that are harmful to ourselves or others. He persuades us to gorge ourselves on synthetic, genetically engineered, irradiated, pesticide-laden foods, and then so distorts our thinking that we blame God for our resulting illness.

He whispers to us that we can wait one more day before we begin a nutritious diet, exercise program, and healthy lifestyle. One more day follows one more day until we run out of days.

Jesus came to liberate the captives. Like this woman, He calls us to Him. "Come over here," He is calling to you. "Come over here. I can see you are hurting. I can see you are bound. Come here and let me help you." He's already won your freedom for you through the shed blood on the Cross. Receive your healing and your liberty now.

*Almighty Heavenly Father, thank You for breaking my chains and lifting my burdens through the shed blood of the Cross. I worship and praise Your Son, Jesus Christ, as my Risen Savior, who has set me free. Thank You for loving me, Father, and for healing me. In Jesus' name, I pray, Amen.*

†

# DAY 52
## GIVE YOUR TESTIMONY

*And one of them, when he saw that he was healed, turned back, and with a loud voice glorified God, And fell down on his face at his feet, giving him thanks: and he was a Samaritan.*

*And Jesus answering said, Were there not ten cleansed? But where are the nine? There are not found that returned to give glory to God, save this stranger.*

*And he said unto him, Arise, go thy way: thy faith hath made thee whole.* (Luke 17:15-19)

*And immediately he received his sight, and followed him, glorifying God: and all the people, when they saw it, gave praise unto God.* (Luke 18:43)

*And he leaping up stood, and walked, and entered with them into the temple, walking, and leaping, and praising God. And all the people saw him walking and praising God.* (Acts 3:8-9)

Notice how many times Scripture tells us about the results of giving your public testimony about your healing or deliverance. It seems obvious that a person would be grateful after he is healed, yet people today are not much different from the ten lepers, only one of whom gave Jesus his thanks, praise, and worship. It is shocking to encounter person after person who has received his healing or deliverance and then to discover that he is not giving his testimony and praising God for being made whole.

121

Gratitude is a vital attitude, and it is one that blesses Father God. It also reminds us that we have not saved ourselves or healed ourselves (even if we have had some medical intervention). God and God alone is the healer, and it is critical that we never let our focus shift from Him.

Giving your testimony often and boldly is part of being a faithful witness to the Lord. Lots of people need to hear your own personal story to give them hope and to show them the way to their own healing. Actually, it is selfish to remain silent and it is quite foolish, too. The Lord said, "Freely you have received; freely give" (Matthew 10:8). In these last days, people desperately need to hear your testimony of the love and the power of our Savior, who is alive and who wants everyone to be saved, healed, delivered, and made whole.

Share your testimony of healing and deliverance. Make a difference in someone's life today.

*Father God, I am sorry I have remained silent when I had opportunities to tell others of my healing and deliverance. This very day I will share my testimony with someone. I thank You, praise You, and glorify Your holy name. In Jesus' name, I pray, Amen.*

† 

# DAY 53
## BELIEVE AND TRUST

*Let not your heart be troubled: ye believe in God, believe also in me.* (John 14:1)

Stop worrying. Trust God. Trust Jesus. Trust in the Holy Spirit. Ten simple words get to the heart of Christian faith.

What is trust all about? The first part of trust is believing. It is believing that God can do what He says He *will* do. And it is believing that God *does* do what He says He *will* do. This level of trust is totally spiritual, and most Christians generally profess to have this faith.

The second part of trust is action. Beliefs are meaningless unless they are manifested in action. Trusting in God means asking God's direction in your daily activities and listening for His answers *before* proceeding.

Let's take a simple example with regard to your health. Suppose your head hurts with an ordinary headache. How many times do you reach for a bottle of painkiller without ever asking God what is the healthiest course of action for you to take?

Now consider something such as a tumor. How many times do you follow medical opinions for a serious or even potentially fatal problem without asking the Great Physician for His instructions as well?

Having received the best medical advice you can obtain, lay down your own opinions and the opinions of others at the feet of Jesus so that you can hear God's voice clearly. Lay down your own logic and that of others, which has only the narrow view of a human being.

Open yourself up to allow God's perfect wisdom to be revealed to you. Then follow exactly what you receive from Him. This is the way to eliminate worry and fear from your life. This is belief in action. This is trust made reality.

*Almighty God, sometimes my mind wanders to my symptoms and my illness, and before I know it, I am worrying about what I see and what I feel in my body. Your Word tells me not to worry, so I take those thoughts captive to the obedience of Christ. I choose to believe You, Father. You are not a man and cannot lie. Your Word is truth, complete truth. I declare my trust in You and in Your Son, Jesus Christ. Today I will LIVE my trust in You and in Your Son, my Savior. You are Jehovah-Rapha, the God who heals me. Your Son healed all who came to Him to be made whole, and He said, "Your faith has made you whole." I believe. I trust. And I receive my healing. Thank You, Father. In Jesus' name, I pray, Amen.*

† 

# Day 54
# Be Wise

*For your obedience is come abroad unto all men. I am glad therefore on your behalf: but yet I would have you wise unto that which is good, and simple concerning evil.* (Romans 16:19)

Be wise about those things that are good. Focus on them and put your attention there. But be simple or uninformed about those things that are not good and are evil.

Paul urges us to be simple concerning evil. What does that mean when applied to your health? There is a balance that is important to maintain. You do not want to be ignorant and fall into the trap of perishing for lack of knowledge (Hosea 4:6). For example, it is beneficial to become wise about the proper functioning of a healthy body. The focus should be on what health is and therefore on what is good.

But on the other hand, you do not want to know so much that you are no longer "simple" and therefore become stuck in unbelief. There are some people who know every detail of their illness (which came from the evil one) and almost nothing of God's Word (which is perfect in its goodness).

They spend large amounts of time examining every detail about their illness which is the evil thing that has happened to them. Focusing on every possible symptom is unwise because it plants so much doubt and unbelief. What happens is that some people say, "Oh, no, is that going to happen to me?" And at the first twinge, they say, "Oh, no, now I'm going into stage three."

The best way to be "wise unto that which is good" is to immerse yourself in Holy Scripture. The Word is given to us to be "profitable for doctrine, for reproof, for correction, for instruction in righteousness that the man of God may be perfect, thoroughly furnished unto all good works" (2 Timothy 3:16-17)

Scripture is our source of truth and it is the sure wisdom on which we can exercise our faith. God says that He upholds His Word and He always fulfills it. By flooding our minds with God's Word and allowing the Holy Spirit to speak to us, we receive more and more revelation and we become wiser and wiser in the things that bring us victory.

*Father God, I want to be wise about those things which are good and simple concerning those things that are evil. I choose to immerse myself in Your Holy Word. I ask the Holy Spirit to reveal His wisdom to me so that I can live a healthy, victorious life that is a good witness. In the mighty name of Jesus, my Lord and Savior, I pray, Amen.*

✝

# DAY 55
# CHRIST HAS REDEEMED YOU
# FROM EVERY CURSE

*Christ hath redeemed us from the curse of the law, being made a curse for us: for it is written, "Cursed is every one that hangeth on a tree:" That the blessing of Abraham might come on the Gentiles through Jesus Christ; that we might receive the promise of the Spirit through faith.  (Galatians 3:13-14)*

We were created with the breath of life of Almighty God, and we were given every good thing according to His will for us.  God placed us in a glorious Garden, filled with wonderful blessings for us.  However, just as was true in heaven, He allowed his creations on earth the right to free will.  God wanted His children to love Him, worship Him, and honor Him not because they had to do so but because they chose to do so.

Adam and Eve couldn't resist the temptation placed before them, so they disobeyed the instructions of the Lord God Almighty.  Thus, the curse fell upon them and every one of their descendants.  Eventually under Moses, God gave the people of Israel a system of laws, which was so impossible to follow that the people realized they needed a Savior.  The Old Testament describes life under the curse and the people's struggle with sin.

God's ultimate solution was to send His Son to redeem us from the curse of the law. Jesus was made the curse for us and He was made sin for us (2 Corinthians 5:21). He bore our sins (1 Peter 2:24) and He bore our sicknesses (Matthew 8:17). Our redemption was full and complete, body, soul, and spirit. No power over us was left to satan either at the spiritual level, the mental level, or the physical level. Forevermore there was to be no more curse (Revelation 22:3) for those who believe in Jesus Christ.

Believe God's Word that this is true. Live your faith. The curse can have no power over you unless you allow it. Sickness cannot remain in your body unless you allow it. The evil one cannot control your life unless you allow him to do so. The Redeemer has been sent and He has won the victory. As a born-again believer, you have a personal Savior who calls you by name and who asks that you follow Him. Glorify Him, praise Him, and receive His healing.

*Dear God, thank You for sending Your Son, Jesus Christ, to redeem me from the curse of the law so that by faith I may receive the promise of the Spirit. Whereas in Adam I sin, in Jesus Christ I am saved. Whereas in Adam I was cursed, in Jesus Christ I am redeemed. Whereas in Adam I am subject to sickness and disease, in Jesus Christ I am healed. I rejoice in the salvation, healing, and deliverance of the new covenant, and I offer myself to You in service according to Your will for my life. In Jesus' name, I pray, Amen.*

✝

## DAY 56
## RAISED FROM THE DEAD

*Now there was at Joppa a certain disciple named Tabitha, which by interpretation is called Dorcas: this woman was full of good works and almsdeeds which she did. And it came to pass in those days, that she was sick, and died: whom when they had washed, they laid her in an upper chamber. ...*

*When he [Peter] was come, they brought him into the upper chamber: and all the widows stood by him weeping, and showing the coats and garments which Dorcas made, while she was with them.*

*But Peter put them all forth, and kneeled down, and prayed; and turning him to the body said, Tabitha, arise. And she opened her eyes: and when she saw Peter, she sat up. And he gave her his hand, and lifted her up, and when he had called the saints and widows, presented her alive.* (Acts 9:36-37, 39-41)

Here we have an amazing story. A woman named Tabitha (also called Dorcas), who was always doing good deeds and helping the poor as her service to the Lord, became ill and died. We are not told any details about what happened to her. All we know is that she was cut short in a productive time of her life.

Peter was summoned, and, when he got to Joppa, he found Dorcas, lying in preparation for burial. He knew that one of the commands that Jesus gave was to raise the dead and he was committed to doing the work of the Lord. Sending everybody out of the room, he got down on his knees and prayed. The breath of life returned to Dorcas, and she got up, healed and well.

Since Peter had to send all the widows out of the room, we can assume that those ladies were filled with unbelief that Dorcas could be raised from the dead. They might not have even been Christians since Scripture does not include the widows in the same category with the saints. At the very least, it seems apparent that they did not have a solid understanding of discipleship which calls us to preach, heal, deliver, and raise from the dead.

The power that Peter tapped is the same today as it was two thousand years ago. Peter had nothing that we don't have. Jesus is looking for faithful disciples who believe and do what He said in Matthew 28:19-20. Answer Jesus' call to preach the good news and "to observe all things whatsoever I have commanded You." That includes expelling demons, laying hands on the sick, and raising the dead, all to the glory of God.

*Father God, I'm not going to let the enemy kill me before I fulfill Your mission and purpose for me. In the name of Jesus, I bind the spirit of death and command him to go. I choose to be a vital, vibrant witness for You and my risen Savior, Jesus Christ. I walk in the victory of the resurrection power of the Cross. In Jesus' name, I pray, Amen.*

†

# Day 57
# All Disease Bows To The Name of Jesus

*Wherefore God also hath highly exalted him, and given him a name which is above every name:*

*That at the name of Jesus every knee should bow, of things in heaven, and things in earth, and things under the earth;*

*And that every tongue should confess that Jesus Christ is Lord, to the glory of God the Father.   (Philippians 2:9-11)*

*And beginning at Moses and all the prophets, he expounded unto them in all the Scriptures the things concerning himself. (Luke 24:27)*

*Then opened he their understanding, that they might understand the Scriptures.   (Luke 24:45)*


The name of Jesus is above every name and every power that has ever existed, exists now, or will ever exist.  Every knee must bow before the name of Jesus.

Remember that diseases have names.  Arthritis must bow to the name of Jesus.  It must yield to the power of the name and the blood.  Cancer must bow to the name of Jesus.  It must yield to the power of the name and the blood.  Diabetes must bow to the name of Jesus.  It must yield to the power of the name above all names and the blood.

Jesus is the Word according to John 1:1. After His resurrection He taught His disciples about the Old Testament Scriptures, showing how He was revealed there. He must have taken them to Exodus and the Passover and shown them that He was the Lamb. He must have taken them to Joshua and shown them that He was the captain. Over and over again He revealed Himself in the Word.

We have the precious Word, the glorious name of Jesus, and the shed blood of the Cross. Father God has given us everything we need. How blessed we are. Lift your voice in songs of thanksgiving that you walk in victory, love, and healing.

*Father God, I confess to Your glory that Jesus Christ is Lord. His is the name above every name and every knee must bow to Him. I thank You that every disease must yield to the power of the Cross. I love Your Word, Father. Help me as I study it so that I will develop a fuller understanding of what being saved, healed, delivered, and made whole really is and how I can be a doer and not a hearer only. Open my understanding, Father, through revelation of the Holy Spirit. In Jesus' name, I pray, Amen.*

✝

# DAY 58
# BLESSED ARE YOU WHO BELIEVE

*And blessed is she that believed: for there shall be a performance of those things which were told her from the Lord.*   (Luke 1:45)

God had a plan to send Jesus as our Savior.  But first, He needed a young woman to take a giant step of faith and to believe what an angel would be sent to tell her.  What if Mary had not accepted what Gabriel said?

Mary was just a young girl, being told news that in many ways was very unwelcome.  Think about her situation.  She was betrothed to Joseph, which in those days was as binding as marriage is today.  The actual marriage ceremony would come later, but the two of them were to be as totally faithful to each other as though they were already married.  The penalty for violating the betrothal promises was to be stoned.

Therefore, when an angel came and said that she was going to be pregnant by the Spirit of God, that was not necessarily good news.  We see the event as magnificent through our eyes of modern-day life.  But to be a young teenager in peril of death by having some preposterous pronouncement by an angel is actually a different story.  It is easy to see why she left immediately for three months because she needed time to get grounded enough to handle the difficulties that would soon come.

The Word says that she did not tell anyone, certainly a wise choice. Can you hear her friends' response to her? "Yeah, right, Mary. An angel said you are going to get pregnant by the Spirit of God. Right. No way, Mary. What *really* happened?"

The first miracle concerning our Lord's birth was not actually Mary's conceiving through the Holy Spirit. It was her belief that God meant what He said. It was in her trusting acceptance that, if God said it, there would certainly be a performance of those things that were told to her from the Lord.

Believe God. And stand in faith that He performs everything He promises that He will do.

*Father God, it is written, blessed is she who believed. I believe, Father. I believe. It is also written that there shall be a performance of those things told to me from the Lord. Through Your Holy Word you tell me that by the stripes of Jesus I was healed. I know that because of the finished work of the Cross, Your healing power is already flowing to me and is constantly available to perform everything that Your Word proclaims. I believe, Father. I stand in faith and I receive. I thank You for my full redemption through salvation, for my healing, for my deliverance, and for my being made whole. No more will I pick and choose which benefit I will accept. With a heart full of gratitude I embrace them all so that I can walk in the victory which You died to give me. I love You, Lord. In the mighty name of Jesus, I pray, Amen.*

†

# DAY 59
# BE A DOER OF THE WORD

*Therefore whosoever heareth these sayings of mine, and doeth them, I will liken him unto a wise man, which built his house upon a rock: and the rain descended, and the floods came, and the winds blew, and beat upon that house; and it fell not: for it was founded upon a rock.* (Matthew 7:24-25)

*But be ye doers of the word, and not hearers only, deceiving your own selves. For if any be a hearer of the word, and not a doer, he is like unto a man beholding his natural face in a glass: for he beholdeth himself, and goeth his way, and straightway forgetteth what manner of man he was.*

*But whoso looketh into the perfect law of liberty, and continueth therein, he being not a forgetful hearer, but a doer of the work, this man shall be blessed in his deed.* (James 1:22-25)

*And they went forth, and preached every where, the Lord working with them, and confirming the word with signs following. Amen.* (Mark 16:20)

Get out and do what I tell you to do, the Lord says to us over and over again. Be a doer of the Word, not just a hearer.

We are doers in two ways. First, having received the understanding of the fullness of what the Greek word "*sozo*" really means, we apply it in our own lives. Just *knowing* this revelation still leaves us sick and in bondage to the enemy unless we *do* what the Word tells us to do. We have to act on it and enforce the Word in our lives. If we don't do that, James tells us that we "forget what manner of man we are."

We are not "only human" through the power of the Lord. We have the Almighty Lord God of the Universe, the Most High God, operating in and through us. With Him all things are possible and nothing is too hard. Hallelujah! These words fill us with God's glory, awe, encouragement, joy, and expectation.

The second way we are doers is by being disciples and carrying the message of salvation, deliverance, and healing to others. We are called to show everyone the vast array of precious gifts that God has provided for us through the shed blood of His Son. And the Word says that the Lord will confirm His Word with signs following (Mark 16:20).

Wholeness! A ministry of wholeness! That is your good news. You are made whole. Every provision has been made. Walk in the victory of the Cross and joyfully proclaim it to those around you.


*Father God, I don't want to be a forgetful hearer. I want to be a doer, with my house built on solid rock. Thank You for blessing me for being a doer. I joyfully share the good news of wholeness. In Jesus' name, I pray, Amen.*

✝

# DAY 60
## PUT GOD FIRST

*But seek ye first the kingdom of God, and his righteousness; and all these things shall be added unto you.* (Matthew 6:33)

*And it shall come to pass, if thou shalt hearken diligently unto the voice of the Lord thy God, to observe and to do all his commandments which I command thee this day, that the Lord thy God will set thee on high above all nations of the earth:*

*And all these blessings shall come on thee, and overtake thee, if thou shalt hearken unto the voice of the Lord thy God.* (Deuteronomy 28:1-2)

Do you find yourself turning to God the most when you are concerned about your health? Can it possibly be that you want healing more than (or at least as much as) you want a relationship with God?

God wants us to walk with Him in divine health and wellness, every day all the time. We develop our relationship with Him first, and that relationship becomes the source of our trust. God already knows us, already loves us, already cherishes us so much that He has us written in the palms of His hands. He is our loving Heavenly Father, who always keeps His promises and His Word.

God insists that we place *Him* first and not our healing or anything we want from Him. For most of us there are times when we feel ourselves tempted to slip into our fears or our drivenness or our despair or our anger. These are the times in which the enemy whispers thoughts of defeat and is trying to control us like a puppet on a string.

We must take swift action and "bring into captivity every thought to the obedience of Christ" (2 Corinthians 10:5). Then we must speak the living Word of God over our life.

Remember that, whenever we are in torment, the devil and his principalities are content. Conversely, when we are peaceful, obedient to God, and secure in the Father's love and power, satan is in torment. The key is to stay focused on God and to maintain an attitude of praise, worship, and gratitude.

God wants to shower you with His blessings and to give you His inheritance. Strengthen your relationship with Him and receive your healing.

*Almighty God, there are times I get caught up in what I want, and I let my focus shift from You to me. Father God, I really do want a close relationship with You. I give You all the praise and all the glory for my life and all the blessings You have given me. I'm going to do better at simply allowing myself to receive Your love and Your grace. In Jesus' name, I pray, Amen.*

† 

# Day 61
## God's Divine Nature

*According as his divine power hath given unto us all things that pertain unto life and godliness, through the knowledge of him that hath called us to glory and virtue:*

*Whereby are given unto us exceeding great and precious promises: that by these ye might be partakers of the divine nature, having escaped the corruption that is in the world through lust. (2 Peter 1:3-4)*

God's Word tells us that God has already given us everything we need for life. These things have *already* been given. They are ours through God's Son, God's covenants, and God's Word. Included in these things that have been provided for us are "exceeding great and precious promises." Peter tells us that one of the benefits of these gifts is that we would be "partakers of the divine nature."

Let your mind consider what it means to be a "partaker of the divine nature." Remember that God created us in the beginning as beings imbued with divine nature because He created us in the likeness and image of Himself. Designed to be His family, we share vital and fundamental aspects of God Himself.

Does divine nature and God's likeness and image include sickness and disease? Of course not. Does illness represent God's will for us? Of course not. If we really believe that it is divine nature for us to be ill and that it is God's will for us to be sick, we would not race to the doctor to be healed. We would not build hospitals and medical schools and laboratories.

To use any of those things if we really believe God wants us to be sick would be to flaunt God's will just as rebelliously as Adam and Eve did when they ate of the fruit of the knowledge of good and evil. Without any doubt, know that sickness is the tool of the devil which destroys God's life force within us and saps our strength and vitality.

Rejoice that through the blood of Jesus you are a partaker of the divine nature. Rejoice in the promises of God's Word. And rejoice that God has given you every good thing.

*Father God, You have given me everything I need for life. You have sent Your Word and Your Son, Jesus Christ, to proclaim Your great and precious promises, and through them I am called to be a partaker of Your divine nature. Thank You for giving me every tool I need to withstand and overcome the attacks of the enemy. I choose to stay focused on Your goodness and glory and healing power. In Jesus' name, I pray, Amen.*

✝

# DAY 62
## FREE WILL

*And the Lord God commanded the man, saying, Of every tree of the garden thou mayest freely eat:*

*But of the tree of the knowledge of good and evil, thou shalt not eat of it: for in the day that thou eatest thereof thou shalt surely die. (Genesis 2:16-17)*

Many people believe that everything that happens in the universe is caused by God. When bad things happen to good people, they believe that God caused the tragedy, accident, or illness for some reason known only to the Almighty and that when they get to heaven they will understand.

The problem with this philosophy is that God's Word clearly states that He allows all His children to have free will. He even allows His angels to have free will. After Lucifer rebelled against God, he was banished from heaven, taking one-third of the angels with him. The evil one and his minions stalk the earth creating disaster in their wake and making every attempt to get us to do likewise. This is not God at work, but the devil at work. When illness strikes, do not blame God for it. Look to the evil one and the ways you have been either vulnerable or cooperative.

God does not want His children to be puppets, incapable of doing anything that He does not control. He wants us to be *real*. He wants us to worship Him because we truly choose to give our hearts to Him and not because He forces us to pay homage to Him.

This passage in Genesis illustrates the freedom that God gave to Adam to make his own choices and to exert his own free will. God told him the consequences of a defiant choice, and He asked for obedience. Therefore, for us obedience is an act of worship, and through it we voluntarily offer our free will back to God and ask Him to direct and use it to His glory.

Remember that no matter what the evil one may do, God can create good from any situation. The enemy has been defeated, and we are supposed to walk in the victorious life that Jesus died to give us. So surrender your will to the Lord, rise up, and live!

*Almighty God, there are times when I struggle with issues of free will. My spirit wants to follow after You, but my soul and my flesh want to do things that I know aren't wise and are contrary to Your will for me. Help me to take control over my thoughts and to obey your instructions cheerfully, willingly, and promptly. Thank You for bringing me victory over all circumstances and restoring peace to my soul no matter what my situation may be. In Jesus' name, I pray, Amen.*

✝

# DAY 63
# THE COMPASSION OF JESUS

*But when he saw the multitudes, he was moved with compassion on them, because they fainted, and were scattered abroad, as sheep having no shepherd.* (Matthew 9:36)

Jesus had been traveling around the countryside, visiting many cities and villages, teaching in their synagogues, proclaiming the good news of the kingdom of God, and curing all kinds of disease and infirmity. He was in action, fulfilling His mission of preaching, delivering, and healing. Healing what? *All* kinds of disease. *Every* weakness and infirmity.

What is the situation described in Matthew 9:36? The Amplified Bible uses these words: "When He saw the throngs, He was moved with pity and sympathy for them, because they were bewildered (harassed and distressed and dejected and helpless), like sheep without a shepherd." What a vivid description!

We think that modern society is unique in its stresses, yet look at this account of people two thousand years ago. Can you relate to feeling bewildered and harassed? To feeling distressed and dejected? To feeling helpless? Many in the crowd felt ill and their illness magnified their anxiety. Sickness can certainly make you feel trapped and stranded, like a lost sheep who has gone astray.

Jesus' message was that God cares for the lost sheep. He has from the beginning. The twenty-third Psalm begins, "The Lord is my Shepherd. I shall not want."

Our loving, Heavenly Father never wants us to suffer any lack of any good thing. God is moved with compassion and sympathy for you, and He has sent Jesus as the Good Shepherd to find you and bring you back to safety. The Good Shepherd does only the will of the Father, and He heals all who come to Him.

Sometimes you may feel faint and scattered inside, overwhelmed by business schedules, housework, financial concerns, meetings, and daily activities. Illness adds more than you think you can bear. Give it all to Jesus, your Shepherd. He calls you gently to Him and enfolds you in His loving, healing arms.

*Merciful Father, thank You for looking on me with compassion. There are times when I feel bewildered and harassed, distressed and dejected. Modern life seems overwhelming and there are many demands on my time and my energy. I rejoice knowing that when I was lost, You found me, and when I was sick, You healed me. You are my Shepherd. In You I find my refuge, my safety, and my healing. With a grateful heart, in Jesus' name, I pray, Amen.*

✝

# Day 64
# God Never Forgets You

*Can a woman forget her sucking child, that she should not have compassion on the son of her womb? Yea, they may forget, yet will I not forget thee. Behold, I have graven thee upon the palms of my hands.* (Isaiah 49:15-16)

What more tender image is there than that of a mother nursing her infant? It is a picture of supreme love, of protection, of nurturing, of caring. Most mothers fulfill the description presented here and love their children with a bond that is the strongest on earth. No one questions the sacrifices that a mother will make to provide for her child and to protect her young.

God tells us that a mother's love pales in comparison to the love He has for us. It is almost incomprehensible for a mother to forget her child. Nevertheless, God uses that as an illustration. "Though *she* may forget you, *I* will not forget you!" He promises. "I will never, ever forget you. See! Come and look! I have engraved you on the palms of my hands."

Stop to think for a moment what it means that God has engraved you on the palms of His hands. It means He has made you a part of Him. It means that it is His will that you never be separated from Him. It means that He wants you to experience everything that living in the presence of the Father Almighty entails.

It means that He is constantly making plans for you. In Jeremiah 29:11, God declares, "For I know the thoughts that I think toward you, ... thoughts of peace, and not of evil [calamity], to give you an expected end [a future and a hope]."

Even though we do not remember it, we all carry within us the sense of being a helpless, vulnerable infant. As adults, when we experience difficult challenges, we may find ourselves feeling those old feelings of helplessness. We may even move away from God. But He will never move away from us and He constantly tries to draw us back to Him.

We have a parent who cannot let us down and whose love for us is so deep and so vast that we cannot comprehend it. This loving Father will never fail us.

*Dear Heavenly Father, whether or not I had a loving, nurturing earthly parent is no longer an issue. What is important is that I now understand how much You love me as Your child. What is important is that I know in the depths of my being that You will not leave me and that You will not fail me. You have engraved me in the palms of Your hands, and, therefore, You carry me with You always. Thank You, God, for being faithful to me and holding me tightly in Your loving arms. In Jesus' name, I pray, Amen.*

# †

# DAY 65
# GOD ALWAYS ANSWERS YOU

*Then shalt thou call, and the Lord shall answer; thou shalt cry, and he shall say, Here I am.  (Isaiah 58:9)*

Isaiah praised the faithfulness and eternal loving presence of Jehovah.  Whatever your problem, he said, "You shall call, and the Lord shall answer; you shall cry, and He shall say, 'Here I am.'"  No matter what your situation is, the Lord God Almighty hears your cry and is present.

Isaiah had only the promise of a Messiah to come.  We live in the glorious fulfillment of that promise.  Jesus has come and Jesus has brought everything to us - salvation, healing, deliverance, and being made whole.  It has already been done for us.  And we do not ever have to wonder if God is here because we have the Holy Spirit dwelling within us every minute of every day.  The Holy Spirit is always present in every born-again believer and never, ever leaves.  Hallelujah!  How blessed we are to live in such a time as this.

If your healing has not manifested yet, remain firm in confessing God's Word, and do not be distracted by satan's lying symptoms.  Spend more time reading Holy Scripture each day, filling your mind with the Word.

Check to make sure that you are not making assumptions about what you should do about your health without first getting guidance from the Holy Spirit. Your assumptions may seem reasonable, but remember, "there is a way that seemeth right unto a man; but the end thereof are the ways of death" (Proverbs 16:25). Keep exploring options and expanding your knowledge. As the Holy Spirit gives you revelation knowledge, be obedient to follow it. Be alert for all forms of direction which God sends to you.

Follow God's health laws to get proper nutrition, adequate exercise, and sufficient rest. Laugh often, glorifying the Lord for His abundant blessings. Develop an attitude of perpetual gratitude, praying prayers of thanksgiving and praise.

Lastly, remember that you are not a failure. God is a faithful God. What He requires is that you remain steadfast and faithful to Him.

*Father God, I rejoice in knowing that You are a faithful God who has already made every provision for me. I love You, Father. And I thank You for sending Your Son Jesus Christ, who took my infirmities and bore my sicknesses and sins on the Cross. It is finished. Your healing power has been released and I receive it now, Father. I am so grateful that the Holy Spirit dwells within me and will never leave me. I rejoice in knowing that I am never alone and am loved with a never-ending love. In Jesus' name, I pray, Amen.*

# † GREAT RESOURCES

## Website for Support and Encouragement

http://www.GodWantsYouToBeWell.com
This is treasure-chest of articles on healing – from explanations of Christ's atonement, to the benefits of music for your healing, to tutorials on Bible study resources.

And perhaps best of all, this is a place to get personal support and prayers from like-minded believers! On this website you can share your own comments and receive encouragement from others. Also be sure to get your free sample of scripture cards. (You can also order the full set.)

## Books and Teaching CDs

1) *Sparkling Gems from the Greek*
2) *Paid in Full, An In-Depth Look at the Defining Moments of Christ's Passion*
3) *A Light in Darkness*
By Rick Renner
Renner Ministries
P.O. Box 702040, Tulsa, OK  74170-2040
918-496-3213
**www.renner.org**

1) *Dismantling Mammon*
2) *Healed: Once And For All*
3) *No More Curse*
4) *Pressed Beyond Measure*
5) *Releasing Seed That Produces Kingdom Dominion*
6) *The Spirit of Victory*
By Pastor Tracy Harris
Harvest International Ministries
4000 Arkansas Boulevard
Texarkana, AR 71854
870-774-4446
www.experiencehim.org


1) *Authority of a Renewed Mind*
2) *Preparations for a Move of God*
3) *The Healing Library*
By Dr. Sandra Kennedy
Sandra Kennedy Ministries
2621 Washington Road, Augusta, GA 30904
706-737-4530
www.sandrakennedy.org


*How to Live and Not Die*
By Norvel Hayes
Norvel Hayes Ministries
P.O. Box 1379, Cleveland, TN 37364
423-476-1018

1) *You've Already Got It*
2) *Believer's Authority*
3) *A Better Way to Pray*
4) *The True Nature of God*
By Andrew Wommack
Andrew Wommack Ministries
P.O. Box 3333, Colorado Springs, CO   80934-3333
719-635-1111
www.awmi.net


1) *Atonement*
2) *You Shall Receive Power*
3) *Blessing or Curse*
4) *The Basics of Deliverance*
By Derek Prince
Derek Prince Ministries
P.O. Box 19501, Charlotte, North Carolina 28219
704-357-3556
www.derekprince.org


*The Blessing of the Lord*
By Kenneth Copeland
Kenneth Copeland Ministries
Fort Worth, TX  76192-0001
800-600-7395
www.kcm.org

*The Tongue – A Creative Force*
*Can Your Faith Fail?*
By Charles Capps
P.O. Box 69
England, AR  72046
501-842-2576
www.charlescapps.org


*Christ the Healer*
By F. F. Bosworth
1973, Fleming H. Revell, division of Baker Book House Co.


## Music – Online, Downloads, CDs

www.soulkeeperradio.com
Soulkeeper Radio.  Streaming peaceful Christian music that will restore, renew, and refresh your soul.  While you are working on your computer, have soothing Christian music playing.  This is a very special website, run by Melissa and Joe Champlion.


www.soulkeepermusic.com
A great website!  The Baby Song, Free Evangelism Song, Free Music and more!  Check out all the things the Champlions have available there.

---

### Free Audio Downloads of Selected Devotions
### From *The Power of God's Word*

---

Several of the devotions from The Power of God's Word series may be heard at Soulkeeper Radio and Soulkeeper Music.

They are available as free downloads from the Soulkeeper Music website. http://soulkeepermusic.com/siteswp/ Select the "Free Devotionals" tab.

---

### Scripture Cards
### For Each Volume of
### *The Power of God's Word* Devotional Series

---

Get Scripture Cards for each volume of *The Power of God's Word*. Post your favorite scriptures where you can see them often, and renew your mind with God's healing Word.

Every set of Scripture cards includes the scriptures discussed in the corresponding volume of *The Power of God's Word*.

Visit: **http://www.PowerOfGodsWord.com** to order.

---

### *The Power of God's Word*
### Christian Devotional Healing Series

---

Please visit **http://www.PowerofGodsWord.com**
If you like this book from The Power of God's Word Series, then you will love the other volumes.

Get the series as:
- Paperback books from Amazon.com
- Digital e-books from Amazon Kindle.
- Digital e-books from Barnes and Nobles Nook.
- Printable e-books in PDF format (immediate download).
- Scripture cards.
- Audio CDs.

Volume 1 – The Power of God's Word for Healing
70 daily devotions!  You will learn:
- Why misunderstanding what the word "saved" means can keep you from being healed.
- Why saying sentences with "I am" can either help you recover or keep you sick.
- Why there is power for healing in communion.
- Why your words determine your health.
- And much more!

Volume 2 – The Power of God's Word for Receiving Healing
65 daily devotions! You will learn:
- Why it is critical to know the difference between facts and the truth.
- Why the unbelief of others can affect your recovery.
- How to look beyond the appearance of your ailments.
- Why not consulting God first can trap you.

Volume 3 – The Power of God's Word for Overcoming Hindrances to Healing
78 daily devotions! You will learn:
- Why misunderstanding Job will keep you sick.
- Why Paul's thorn was not sickness.
- Why suffering sickness does not glorify God.
- Why it is almost impossible to be healed if you don't do three important things.
- How to pray effective prayers instead of prayers that actually hinder your recovery.

Volume 4 – The Power of God's Word for Healthy Living
73 daily devotions! You will learn:
- Five easy habits to develop to promote your health.
- Why herbs and essential oils are God's blessings for healing.
- Three emotions that are critical for good health.
- Why it matters what music you listen to.
- Why some kinds of meditation hurt you instead of helping you.

## A Gift for You

Our Thank You to you! We have a gift of some free Scripture cards for you!

Please visit this website to receive your free Scripture cards: **http://www.PowerOfGodsWord.com/gft-two** .

## End Notes

Cover photograph by Janice Waltzer
    www.flickr.com
    License: Attribution 2.0 Generic (CC BY 2.0)

22027002R00083